# The Rôle of the Teacher
### in the
# Nursery School

*by*

JOAN E. CASS

*formerly Lecturer in Child Development,*
*The Institute of Education, London University*

## PERGAMON PRESS

OXFORD · NEW YORK · TORONTO
SYDNEY · PARIS · BRAUNSCHWEIG

| U. K. | Pergamon Press Ltd., Headington Hill Hall, Oxford OX3 0BW, England |
|---|---|
| U. S. A. | Pergamon Press Inc., Maxwell House, Fairview Park, Elmsford, New York 10523, U.S.A. |
| CANADA | Pergamon of Canada, Ltd., 207 Queen's Quay West, Toronto 1, Canada |
| AUSTRALIA | Pergamon Press (Aust.) Pty. Ltd., 19a Boundary Street, Rushcutters Bay, N.S.W. 2011, Australia |
| FRANCE | Pergamon Press SARL, 24 rue des Ecoles, 75240 Paris, Cedex 05, France |
| WEST GERMANY | Pergamon Press GmbH, 3300 Braunschweig, Postfach 2923, Burgplatz 1, West Germany |

Copyright © 1975 Joan E. Cass

First edition 1975

Library of Congress Catalog Card No. 75-19414

**Library of Congress Cataloging in Publication Data**

Cass, Joan E
The role of the teacher in the nursery school.

(Pergamon international library of science, technology, engineering, and social studies)
Bibliography: p.
1. Education, Preschool. 2. Nursery school teachers. I. Title.
LB1140.2.C373      372.1'1'02      75-19414
ISBN 0 08 018282 8
ISBN 0 08 018281 X flexi

*Printed in Great Britain by A. Wheaton & Co. Exeter*

# Dedication

I would like to dedicate this book to all the members of my tutorial groups when I was a lecturer in the Department of Child Development, Institute of Education, London University. I learnt so much from them and enjoyed their company enormously.

*What do you live for?*
(D. H. Lawrence)

# Contents

# Foreword

Some of the material contained in this book has come from *The Rôle of the Teacher in the Infant and Nursery School.* This book was written by Miss Dorothy E. M. Gardner and myself. Since Miss Gardner's death the book has gone out of print and I was asked if I would consider preparing a new edition. In looking at the material I knew that I could only take out and deal with the part that I myself had contributed, i.e. on the rôle of the teacher in the nursery school, as I had had no part in the main section of the book which dealt with the infant school teacher. I have, however, added several extra chapters which I felt were important at this stage.

Perhaps in the future someone else will be able to rearrange the excellent material which Miss Gardner wrote and edited. Obviously the feel and flavour of the present book will be very different from the original edition as it is written in my own style and in the way I see the situation and present-day needs, but I hope it may prove useful and enjoyable reading.

# Acknowledgements

I should like to thank the many people who have helped in providing much of the material contained in this book. First of all the observers (all trained, experienced teachers studying in the Department of Child Development, Institute of Education, London University) for their careful and thorough investigations into the subject and particularly Miss Brenda Page (late headmistress of a London nursery school) whose original study inspired others to continue with the work; and also Dr. Ilse Hellman, at one time on the staff of the Child Development Department, for the assistance she gave Miss Page in the early stages of the study.

Then the heads and assistant teachers who so generously accepted the observers in their schools, giving them all the information they needed, and the many local authorities that allowed observations to be made in their schools.

I am also very grateful to Miss Kay Edgar for the material in Chapter 5, "The rôle of the teacher in the co-operation between home and nursery school" from her unpublished thesis, and Miss Kathleen Carrington for her contribution in Chapter 7 on "The rôle of the teacher in caring with the handicapped child", also from her unpublished thesis.

I am very fortunate in having friends in the educational world, ready and willing to read the completed manuscript, and I would like to thank Mr. Brian Seagrove, Lecturer in Education, for many helpful corrections and comments, and Mrs. Margaret Grubbe, Head of a London nursery school, for supplying information in Chapter 8 dealing with the nursery school teacher and her assistant. I am very grateful to Mr. Brian Seagrove for reading the proofs for me.

No one, of course, can take responsibility for the book as a whole except myself.

# CHAPTER 1

# Introduction

*Tempora mutantur, nos et mutamur in illis.*

How has our conception of the nursery school changed and developed during the years since it began, and how, therefore has the rôle and function of the teacher in relation to the children in her care, altered to suit present-day society?

Nursery schools started in this country as a remedy for bad social conditions. Young children were living in dirty, overcrowded homes, denied the good food, sleep, medical care, fresh air, and sunshine they so badly needed.

One of the main arguments of Margaret McMillan in her fight for nursery schools was the deplorable health of the children on entry into the infant schools when they were found to be suffering from so many preventable ills. This meant that the early nursery schools felt that the health of the young child was the first consideration, and the simple buildings devised were planned so that children got the maximum amount of fresh air and sunshine. Cleanliness was very important in those early days, and children were often bathed and spent a lot of time in washing or cleaning their teeth, while the formation of good habits were considered vital. A well-planned midday meal with morning milk and often something to eat before going home helped to make up for a poor and insufficient home diet.

The emphasis on fresh air and sunshine meant that children spent a lot of time out of doors, and the buildings were planned for this purpose; in fact, the "in and out" play which this involved is still a very important feature of nursery school life.

The nursery school day was often a very long one, as it was felt that the more time a child spent away from his insanitary home the better; nor was the nursery school really considered as the right of every child; those living

1

under more favourable conditions could well manage in their own homes until old enough for school.

Although the nursery school as a younger institution than the infant school was never thought of as just a purveyor of information or moral training, the daily programme was much more formal than it is today. Apart from the carefully organized toilet and washing periods, which took up quite a lot of time, it was also felt that children from disorganized and haphazard homes needed a well-planned day with plenty of sense-training apparatus for them to use, careful group experiences, the cultivation of good, clean habits, and a long sleep on stretcher beds in the afternoon if they were really going to benefit from their time in the nursery school.

Gradually, of course, social conditions did improve, and our knowledge of child development grew as the result of experience and research in this country and the United States. Children were recognized as individuals, and their all-round mental health, their emotional, social, and intellectual development was seen to be as important as their physical well-being. Many parents from more privileged homes realized the value of nursery school education and wanted their children to attend. Although some children lived in seemingly comfortable homes well provided with many of the luxuries of life, this did not mean that their all-round development was being satisfactorily catered for. Such children were often deprived of space to play, a rich play environment and companionship, and sometimes had parents who were neglectful or over-indulgent. In order to help more children, and because of (1) the emphasis on the mother—child relationship, (2) living standards had improved so that many children no longer needed to spend long hours away from their own homes, and (3) the midday meal and the afternoon rest were no longer considered quite so essential, part-time nursery school education was introduced. This meant children attending either for every morning or every afternoon.

There still remained, of course, many young children who still needed the benefit of longer hours, and so a number of nursery schools today have both full-time and part-time children in the same group, though there are others which work on a wholly part-time basis.

In some ways having two groups of children adds to the work of the teacher. If she has a group of 20 or 25 children in the morning and another similar group in the afternoon, she has to get to know intimately about 50 children and their parents. Each group will make demands on her energy, skill, ingenuity, patience, and understanding, and it will involve starting each afternoon with the same vitality and enthusiasm as she brought to her morning group.

Both parents and teachers have mixed feelings about part-time education at the pre-school stage. Some parents feel they would rather their children had the full day at nursery school where they are sure they will get and eat a well-balanced midday meal and they themselves will have more time for all their family and household jobs. Some teachers, too, miss the intimacy of the midday meal and the afternoon play, and find it more difficult to get to know and understand the needs and problems of 40 or 50 young children, though this does depend on the individual parent or teacher.

Smaller groups, a very flexible programme, much less emphasis on habit training, more time for exciting and challenging play, and all sorts of new play materials make new demands on teachers. More research into the problems and needs of young children, which involves more reading, attendance at refresher courses, the keeping, perhaps, of careful records, co-operation with a number of outside agencies, visits from many interested bodies, the presence of students in training, closer contacts with the children's families — all these tend to make the teacher's rôle a very skilled, exacting, and influential one today, requiring careful training, ability, and maturity.

CHAPTER 2

# The Object of this Study

*What is the price of experience? Do men buy it for a song or*
*wisdom for a dance in the streets? No, it is bought with the price of*
*all that a man hath.*

(William Blake)

The idea of this particular study was to see if it would be feasible to discover and measure those qualities of personality which the good nursery school teacher seems to possess in such abundance and which obviously affects so significantly the well-being and happiness of the children in her care. What does constitute the teacher's contribution to the social climate of the group of children of whom she is in charge? One has often seen groups of young children similar in age range, in physical environment, and material equipment, and yet very different in social climate. Obviously the difference must lie in the personality of the teacher herself, for a child's emotional tone, his feelings about himself, his self-confidence and self-respect, and his sense of security are deeply affected by the adults' attitude and behaviour towards him, and this in turn will, of course, affect his behaviour towards others.

The example a teacher sets is often far more important than she herself realizes: young children particularly tend to take on the values and behaviour of those they are with. Children are, of course, individuals, the majority of whom are nurtured within the setting of their own families, and the quality of the relationships which they form with adults and other children outside the home and their mental health as a whole will depend to a very large extent on that which they experience within the family.

Some children will obviously find it more difficult than others to make happy and secure relationships and to develop into stable human beings because of both environmental and inherited factors. Although the home is the place which influences the child most, everyone with whom he comes in contact will make some kind of contribution to his development

— a positive or negative one. Therefore the personality of the teacher with whom children often spend a considerable part of the day, particularly perhaps at the nursery school stage when they are so dependent on the adult for support and understanding, will be of extreme importance.

A teacher's work and influence does not consist merely in providing factual material for children to absorb. True education embraces all aspects of development — emotional, social, physical, as well as intellectual. A teacher's influence, too, so often extends from the child to his family, for she is aware how inseparable the two are. So knowledge is shared, confidences are built up, and warm, friendly contacts are established and maintained, so that home and nursery school work together for the child's ultimate well-being.

This demands wisdom and maturity from the teacher. Lois Barclay Murphey in her monograph *Social Behaviour and Child Personality* emphasizes this point when she says that anyone who has watched different groups of children is aware of the way in which a happy and affectionate adult can unconsciously release warm friendliness in a group of children and how adult tensions and anxieties may create insecurity and, with it, antagonistic and competitive behaviour in children. It was to try and define and measure these qualities in the individual teacher to which children respond with obvious feelings of well-being and satisfaction and to measure also, where possible, those subtle qualities of temperament — such things as a teacher's vitality, spontaneity, buoyancy, and gaiety, which exert their unconscious influence on children — that this particular study was devised.

To list the actual qualities desirable in a teacher is not, perhaps, such an impossible task. Arthur Jersild in his book *When Teachers Face Themselves* stresses the importance of self-awareness when he points out that the function of good education is to help a growing child to know and accept himself. Nor can a teacher help children in this respect if they do not know and understand themselves also. Otherwise they will continue to see those they teach through the bias and distortions of their own unrecognized needs, fears, guilts, anxieties, and hostile impulses. So the process of gaining knowledge of self and the struggle for satisfaction and self-fulfilment is not something taught but that in which the individual himself is involved.

Susan Isaacs in *The Psychological Aspects of Child Development* points out that it is "highly desirable that the educators of young children should have sufficient understanding of the psychological processes underlying the difficulties of behaviour to be able to exercise patience and understanding so that they realize that time and normal growth under favourable conditions will do much to relieve these difficulties".

Nathan Isaacs in his pamphlet *What is Required of the Nursery Infant Teacher in the Country Today?* sees the teacher's task as "recognizing the importance of the individual and the principle of respect for each person's integrity with the fact that we are forced to impose a certain pre-chosen pattern as a child grows into the life and the likeness of the society of which he forms a part so that we must try to achieve the optimal reconciliation of the social steering the child needs with the shaping he cannot escape, with respect for his integrity".

The Nursery and Infant School Report* stipulates that: "The first essential for a teacher of young children is that she should have the right temperament. A teacher of young children should not only have real love and respect for children, but should be a person of imaginative understanding, sympathy and balance."

Dr. Wall in his Convocation Lecture *Child of Our Times* given to the National Children's Homes (1959) emphasizes the need for socialization. Not only that children recognize (though it may be a slow process) the needs of others and adopt a reasonable standard of behaviour of giving and receiving, of co-operation, of affection and love, but that they also gain some insight into their own motives of behaviour and the prejudices of others and that in an informal way they are helped to verbalize and to acknowledge their own and others' behaviour. This will certainly need great skill and understanding on the part of the teacher, and underlines the importance of selection and training.

There are numerous other writers who describe what the good teacher should know and be. The problem, however, which we set ourselves here was in actually observing a living human being, a teacher, with a group of real flesh-and-blood children and in seeing and measuring those personal qualities and techniques which are felt to be really desirable, and in interpreting them in relation to the children concerned.

---

*Report of Consultative Committee, Ministry of Education, HMSO, London, 1933.

# CHAPTER 3

# Methods of Procedure

*The lay of the land is responsible for the flow of the stream*
(Claudine Lewis)

The method eventually selected to try to find what constituted the teacher's contribution to the social climate of a group and to express this quantitatively as far as possible was to observe and time-sample individual teachers whose groups of children were felt to be, as judged by several experienced people, happy and secure. The teachers were chosen (in consultation with the heads) because they appeared to be understanding and sensitive to children's needs, able to give and receive affection, provide a rich environment, and to have sufficient experience to give them confidence in their own judgement. No teacher in her first year out of college was selected, although those chosen differed in age, length of training, and experience. Harold H. Anderson and Helen and J. M. Brewer of Illinois, in their book *Studies of Teacher's Classroom Personalities,* state that they had found that records of 300—400 minutes of observation appeared to give a generally reliable picture of an individual teacher's personality. Therefore in our observations of the 18 nursery school teachers we were able to select, it was decided to record as far as possible what they said and did for 75 minutes on each of 4 days. The results are given in Tables 1—4 at the end of this chapter. A preliminary visit was paid, lasting for a whole morning, in order that the observer might become familiar with the general pattern and routine of the group, the building and equipment available, and the teacher's voice and manner.

There were, of course, a number of practical difficulties.

It was essential that the teacher was untroubled by what was taking place; that she was not, in fact, aware that what she said and did with the children was being recorded. One or two teachers did actually discover that they were being observed, but they were confident and secure people and it did not really worry them. The nursery school teacher is also rarely in one place for any length of time. She moves freely from playroom to garden, from cloakroom to toilet or corridor, and to follow her without arousing her anxieties or getting in her way, and to hear all that she said was obviously out of the question. Nor was it always possible either to see, hear, or record what was involved in the inflexion of a voice, the expression on a face, the movement of a hand, or a spontaneous gesture, or any of those indefinable contacts which make up the personality of the individual and which must, therefore, have their effect upon children. Ideally, too, it would have been good to have been able to protect these selected teachers from distractions and interruptions which prevented them from giving their full attention to their children all the time. However, this was a reality situation, and the hazards involved by the occasional absence of a helper, or the time taken up by the appearance of the school nurse or a visitor, had to be accepted. It happened to all the teachers observed at one time or another. It would have been interesting to have made some of the observations during the midday meal or in a story or music time. It was felt, however, that the play period would be the most fruitful and satisfactory, so all the observations were made then.

It is easy to recognize the importance of the teacher at times when she has gathered children together for some specific activity, to tell them a story, to provide music for them to sing or move to, to serve the midday meal, and preside at the lunch table. The play period, however, is often less easily recognized as a time when the rôle of the teacher is of the utmost importance and when all her skill is needed in guiding, enriching, and providing for the all-round growth, needs, and experiences of the children in her care.

All the teachers were working in well-equipped playrooms generally with "family groupings", i.e. with children from 2 to 5 years of age, though the proportion of 2-year-old children was very, very small, and in some groups there were none at all. The size of the groups varied somewhat, depending on the daily attendance, but it was generally between 20 and 25, and the time of the year when the observations were made also varied somewhat from teacher to teacher.

The classification of contacts in the time-samples made in analysing the teacher's remarks and approaches to the children were those selected in the first year of the study. To these observations certain additions were made as they were found to occur during subsequent observations. Those which proved to be most significant were those which were observed from the beginning. It will be noted that some of these contacts relate to more than one situation, e.g. a teacher may give affection, comfort, etc. In the examples given, however, it should be clear as to which specific situation they refer, though the actual interpretation of what it signified to the child is much more subtle and less easy to define. It is often difficult, for example, to distinguish between "giving help" and "showing care for comfort", between "asking help" and "contributing an interest" by "making a suggestion" or "giving a command". One really needs to know the children very well indeed to be able to decide whether, in fact, a contact was "a giving" or "a taking away". Help at one moment to one child might be a gift, the building up of a relationship; but for another child the withdrawing or the withholding of help might be an assumption of the ability to be independent, and might therefore be the more positive approach, though less obvious as such to the observer. The impinging of one contact on another, the categories chosen, the actual order in which they have been placed, and their interpretation are, of course, open to question. At the moment of impact when the observer put her contact into a particular category, added nothing, and interpreted it in a particular way, it seemed the right thing to do. When the material had been assembled it was worked over again, and as a result some of the categories have been combined where one or two of the original ones appeared to overlap extensively. Otherwise it was judged to be wiser to leave the original ones unchanged as they seemed, on the whole, to represent different aspects of the nursery school teachers' way of helping the children.

*TABLE 1. Contacts made by the teachers*

| Description | Total number of contacts |
|---|---|
| *Group I(a) (concerned with intellectual stimulus of the imparting of information)* | |
| 1. Contributes categorical information, provides intellectual information, ideas, confirms, invites conformation of information from the child | 1560 |
| 2. Invites spontaneous information and ideas from the child | 891 |
| 3. Clarifies a situation by explanation, explains the nature of materials, her own activities and the reasons for her questions, requests, refusals, and actions | 828 |
| 4. Spontaneously offers help, materials, permission, or information | 513 |
| 5. Stimulates the child's interest or draws the child's attention to something new | 276 |
| 6. Corrects child's information, speech, or manners | 89 |

*TABLE 1 – Continued*

| Description | Total number of contacts |
|---|---|
| 7. Questions child to help him solve a problem | 146 |
| 8. Questions or comments on the child's ideas, information, or materials | 89 |
| *Group I(b) (concerned with materials)* | |
| 9. Reminds the child of the use and care of equipment | 6 |
| *Group II(a) (physical care, protection, and comfort)* | |
| 10. Gives affection, comfort, personal attention, or assurance | 519 |
| 11. Warns the child of danger | 185 |
| 12. Suggests the child asks help from his mother | 4 |
| *Group II(b)* | |
| 13. Grants immediately the child's request for help, objects, attention, or permission | 535 |
| 14. Shows admiration for or interest in a child's clothes, possessions, or productions, or confidence in the child's relatives or interest in his home life | 533 |
| 15. Shares child's feelings and imaginative play, laughter, talk, or jokes | 361 |
| 16. Greets or draws a child into a social situation | 207 |
| 17. Shows pleasure in a child's presence or interest in his personal condition | 156 |
| 18. Unspoken, friendly contacts | 7 |
| *Group II(c) (promoting social attitudes)* *(i) By direct means* | |
| 19. Asks or invites a child's help or co-operation, or draws attention to the child's ability to help himself | 773 |
| 20. Contacts likely to promote a good social attitude or an increase in social awareness by any of the following means: recognizing or promoting co-operation suggesting that one child offers or gives, asks, or accepts help from another suggesting that one child invites another to play with him pointing out the discomfort of one child to another reminding the children that others have feelings | 695 |
| 21. Demands a child's help or co-operation | 178 |
| 22. Agrees to grant requests for objects, help, or permission after postponement | 149 |
| 23. Thanks a child for help or gift | 145 |
| 24. Arbitrates in a dispute | 123 |
| 25. Refuses a child's help, gifts, or production | 39 |
| 26. Accepts child's help or gifts | 37 |
| *(ii) By example* | |
| 27. Apologizes to the child | 34 |
| 28. Asks child's permission | 1 |

*Group III(a) (observes children: this was not separately recorded)*

*TABLE 1 — Continued*

| Description | Total number of contacts |
|---|---|
| *Group III(b) (praise and encouragement)* | |
| 29. Accepts a child's information and ideas | 717 |
| 30. Encourages the child by admiration or approval of an achievement or production | 334 |
| 31. Encourages child by suggestion | 281 |
| 32. Comments on child's behaviour | 132 |
| 33. Encourages by reassurance | 110 |
| *Group III(c) (discipline and control)* | |
| 34. Reminds a child of a routine activity | 441 |
| 35. Gives a child a specific order | 399 |
| 36. Reproaches a child for behaviour, untidiness, or noise | 299 |
| 37. Refuses or deflects child's request for help, objects, attention, or permission | 146 |
| 38. Checks child's activity | 20 |
| 39. Ignores child's remark or action | 19 |
| 40. Rejects suggestions or reminds child of an acceptable form of behaviour | 5 |
| *Group IV (when not in direct contact with children in her class)* | |
| 41. Meditates aloud | 155 |
| 42. Seeks adult co-operation, asks or gives information to adult | 27 |
| 43. Mentions child to adult in child's presence | 18 |
| 44. Mentions child to adult in the hearing of other children | 15 |
| 45. Exclamations by the teacher | 10 |

*TABLE 2. Number of contacts made by the individual teachers in the 45 categories*

| | A | B | Ċ | D | E | F | G | H | I | J | K | L | M | N | O | P | Q | R | Total number of categories |
|---|---|---|---|---|---|---|---|---|---|---|---|---|---|---|---|---|---|---|---|
| 1 | 148 | 81 | 189 | 194 | 95 | 55 | 52 | 91 | 34 | 84 | 55 | 63 | 68 | 98 | 64 | 95 | 79 | 108 | 1560 |
| 2 | 48 | 36 | 111 | 45 | 32 | 36 | 30 | 29 | 22 | 23 | 36 | 54 | 33 | 30 | 45 | 72 | 121 | 88 | 891 |
| 3 | 61 | 63 | 135 | 62 | 55 | 17 | 19 | 26 | 35 | 65 | 8 | 45 | 34 | 24 | 39 | 45 | 52 | 43 | 829 |
| 4 | 62 | 65 | 35 | 39 | 33 | 30 | 8 | 22 | 11 | 22 | 5 | 31 | 23 | 19 | 36 | 44 | 22 | 6 | 513 |
| 5 | 29 | 45 | 8 | 24 | 29 | 19 | 14 | 13 | 11 | 7 | – | 26 | 11 | 23 | 12 | 3 | 1 | 1 | 276 |
| 6 | 16 | 8 | 12 | 21 | 12 | 2 | 4 | 5 | 2 | 13 | 3 | 4 | 8 | 17 | 10 | 3 | – | 17 | 157 |
| 7 | 19 | 15 | 6 | 12 | 16 | 2 | 3 | 3 | 3 | 7 | 6 | 6 | 12 | 5 | 7 | 5 | 9 | 10 | 146 |
| 8 | 10 | 8 | 6 | 22 | 23 | 2 | 1 | 1 | 3 | 2 | 1 | – | 1 | – | 1 | 3 | 4 | 1 | 89 |
| 9 | – | – | – | – | – | – | – | – | – | – | – | – | – | – | – | 8 | 1 | – | 9 |
| 10 | 9 | 29 | 40 | 10 | 10 | 35 | 10 | 25 | 39 | 58 | 15 | 26 | 60 | 41 | 46 | 25 | 27 | 4 | 519 |
| 11 | – | – | – | – | – | 7 | 12 | 4 | 27 | 17 | 21 | 32 | 18 | 15 | 18 | 3 | 4 | 7 | 185 |
| 12 | – | – | – | – | – | – | – | – | – | – | – | – | – | – | – | – | 4 | – | 4 |
| 13 | 55 | 49 | 31 | 43 | 19 | 10 | 8 | 8 | 6 | 27 | 7 | 30 | 19 | 22 | 30 | 73 | 40 | 58 | 535 |
| 14 | 51 | 67 | 132 | 45 | 22 | 21 | 5 | 19 | 10 | 4 | 15 | 9 | 28 | 12 | 14 | 37 | 20 | 22 | 533 |
| 15 | 24 | 45 | 32 | 37 | 34 | 16 | 13 | 50 | 10 | 11 | 15 | 13 | 7 | 7 | 5 | 7 | 16 | 19 | 361 |
| 16 | 19 | 19 | 28 | 18 | 4 | 5 | 1 | 5 | 4 | 5 | 7 | 4 | 13 | 5 | 10 | 32 | 10 | 11 | 207 |
| 17 | 20 | 20 | 29 | 13 | 14 | 3 | 4 | 9 | 5 | 5 | 2 | 1 | 8 | 4 | 11 | 3 | 6 | 9 | 156 |
| 18 | – | – | – | – | – | – | – | – | – | – | – | – | – | 1 | – | – | – | 6 | 7 |
| 19 | 31 | 35 | 55 | 22 | 20 | 40 | 26 | 63 | 27 | 50 | 25 | 78 | 65 | 53 | 81 | 26 | 32 | 44 | 773 |
| 20 | 36 | 41 | 149 | 30 | 28 | 19 | 17 | 25 | 31 | 33 | 16 | 59 | 72 | 72 | 33 | 16 | 7 | 11 | 695 |
| 21 | – | – | – | – | – | 3 | 3 | 2 | 7 | 14 | 1 | – | 3 | – | – | 16 | 31 | 98 | 178 |
| 22 | 19 | 7 | 20 | 4 | 12 | 5 | 1 | 13 | 2 | 18 | 2 | 3 | 5 | 8 | 9 | 9 | 5 | 7 | 149 |
| 23 | 3 | 8 | 14 | 5 | 1 | 9 | 3 | 8 | 7 | 18 | 5 | 5 | 13 | 11 | 15 | 4 | 4 | 12 | 145 |
| 24 | – | – | – | – | – | 3 | 12 | 6 | 4 | 8 | 9 | 29 | 13 | 15 | 14 | 7 | 2 | 1 | 123 |
| 25 | 1 | 2 | 3 | 1 | 3 | 3 | 6 | 4 | – | 3 | – | 3 | 2 | 4 | 3 | – | 1 | – | 39 |
| 26 | 5 | 3 | 1 | 2 | 2 | 2 | – | 2 | – | – | – | 4 | 2 | 2 | 0 | 1 | 1 | 4 | 37 |
| 27 | – | – | – | – | – | 1 | 1 | 1 | – | 4 | 2 | 6 | 5 | 2 | 5 | 2 | 4 | 1 | 34 |
| 28 | – | – | – | – | – | – | – | – | – | – | – | – | – | – | – | 1 | – | – | 1 |
| 29 | 31 | 44 | 115 | 77 | 23 | 12 | 2 | 22 | 12 | 28 | 8 | 9 | 26 | 14 | 30 | 112 | 91 | 61 | 717 |
| 30 | – | – | – | – | – | 38 | 25 | 51 | 8 | 29 | 16 | 28 | 37 | 12 | 31 | 38 | 3 | 18 | 334 |
| 31 | – | – | – | – | – | 38 | 21 | 26 | 34 | 24 | 10 | 30 | 29 | 29 | 20 | 11 | 5 | 4 | 281 |
| 32 | 14 | 9 | 9 | 20 | 5 | 12 | 2 | 4 | 4 | 8 | 6 | 1 | 18 | 9 | 5 | 5 | 1 | – | 132 |
| 33 | – | – | – | – | – | 14 | 7 | 7 | 11 | 16 | 12 | 9 | 10 | 11 | 10 | 3 | – | – | 110 |
| 34 | 60 | 64 | 44 | 48 | 51 | 21 | 2 | 12 | 17 | 4 | 10 | 23 | 27 | 21 | 28 | – | 3 | 6 | 441 |
| 35 | – | – | – | – | – | 44 | 34 | 29 | 55 | 59 | 17 | 23 | 70 | 22 | 22 | 8 | 10 | 6 | 399 |
| 36 | – | – | – | – | – | 29 | 20 | 3 | 34 | 30 | 23 | 15 | 34 | 20 | 11 | 2 | 3 | 5 | 229 |
| 37 | – | – | – | – | – | 24 | 15 | 29 | 8 | 27 | 4 | 17 | 4 | 14 | 3 | – | – | 1 | 146 |
| 38 | – | – | – | – | – | – | – | – | – | – | – | – | – | – | – | 12 | 2 | 6 | 20 |
| 39 | – | – | – | – | – | – | 1 | 1 | 1 | 4 | 3 | – | – | – | 5 | 2 | 1 | 1 | 19 |
| 40 | – | – | – | – | – | – | – | – | – | – | – | – | – | – | – | 2 | – | 3 | 5 |
| 41 | 5 | 8 | 16 | 19 | 28 | 4 | 5 | 3 | 4 | 2 | 13 | 13 | 7 | 7 | 17 | 1 | – | 3 | 155 |
| 42 | – | – | – | – | – | – | – | – | – | – | – | – | – | – | – | 12 | – | 15 | 27 |
| 43 | – | – | – | – | – | – | – | 3 | 4 | – | 7 | 2 | 2 | – | – | – | – | – | 18 |
| 44 | – | – | – | – | – | – | – | – | 1 | – | 6 | 3 | 1 | 3 | – | – | – | 1 | 15 |
| 45 | – | – | – | – | – | – | – | – | – | – | – | – | – | – | – | 6 | 2 | 2 | 10 |

*TABLE 3. Order of teachers and their
full number of contacts*

| Teacher | Contacts |
|---------|----------|
| C | 1220 |
| D | 813 |
| M | 788 |
| B | 771 |
| P | 754 |
| J | 729 |
| R | 717 |
| L | 701 |
| O | 690 |
| A | 676 |
| N | 650 |
| Q | 627 |
| H | 624 |
| F | 581 |
| E | 571 |
| I | 493 |
| K | 391 |
| G | 387 |

*TABLE 4. Examples of the contacts made by the teachers*

| Description | Total number of contacts from the 18 teachers |
|-------------|-----------------------------------------------|
| 1. Contributes categorical information, provides intellectual information and ideas, confirms and invites confirmation from the child<br>*Teacher:* "We haven't got Susie today, have we?"<br>*Child:* "Good job she hasn't got Asian 'flu."<br>*Teacher:* "No, she hasn't got 'flu, she's going to have a new pair of shoes."<br>*Teacher to child building a canal:* "We can't run the water right down the canal because of the grid."<br>*Teacher:* "Do you know what that colour is? It's prussian blue, that's dark blue." | 1560 |
| 2. Invites spontaneous information and ideas from child<br>*Child:* "Miss X, come and look at my picture."<br>*Teacher, looking at painting:* "Oh, that's lovely, who is that? *(pointing to a figure)*?"<br>*Child:* "My Mummy."<br>*Teacher:* "Your Mummy's very pretty." | 891 |
| 3. Clarifies a situation by explanation, explains the nature of materials, her own activities, and the reasons for her questions, requests, refusals, and actions | 828 |

*TABLE 4 – Continued*

| Description | Total number of contacts from the 18 teachers |
|---|---|
| *Teacher:* "Jane, please keep your feet off the seat, people will get their clothes dirty from your muddy shoes." A child was talking about her brother having a "side pencil": *Teacher:* "A side pencil. Do you mean with a clip on it to fix it in his pocket?" *Teacher refuses to put up a child's drawing:* "Our walls are getting full – I will have to take some down to put more up." | |
| 4. Spontaneously offers help, materials, permission, information *Teacher:* "When you go to the park, you may run as fast as you like." *Child:* "Miss X, we are going to make a tunnel for this red bus." *Teacher:* "Yes, that's right and you can take the big bricks." | 513 |
| 5. Stimulates the child's interest or draws the child's attention to something new *Teacher:* "Aren't these lovely pictures? Look, this is a car." *Child (showing a finished picture):* "Look at this." *Teacher:* "Oh, that is nice! Now would you like something fresh from the cupboard." *Teacher:* "Who wants to play football?" | 276 |
| 6. Corrects child's information, speech, manners Child interrupts. *Teacher:* "Sorry dear, wait until I've finished speaking." *Child, running over to teacher, holding a penny:* "I got a sixpence!" *Teacher:* "Sixpence? No, not a sixpence; a penny." | 157 |
| 7. Questions child to help solve a problem Child puts on a scarf. *Teacher:* "Do you need that on this morning? You think about it." *Teacher:* "What is this colour?" *Child:* "Orange." *Teacher:* "And this one (*child hesitates*), what colour is grass?" *Child:* "Green." *Teacher:* "Green, that's right." | 146 |
| 8. Questions or comments on the child's ideas, information or materials *Child, showing a box:* "Look! There's nothing inside." *Teacher:* "Nothing inside? Yes, there is." | 89 |
| 9. Reminds the child of the use and care of equipment *Teacher:* "Be careful, we don't want to break the doll; hold her nicely." *Child:* "No, I mustn't break her, she's so pretty. I'll put her in the doll's bed and cover her up." | 6 |

*TABLE 4 — Continued*

| Description | Total number of contacts from the 18 teachers |
|---|---|
| *Teacher to child looking at a book:* "Do you remember how I showed you how to turn over the pages?" *Child:* "Yes, like this, I know now." | |
| 10. Gives affection, comfort, personal attention, or assurance *Teacher to child who has fallen down:* "Oh, not very bad, Barry, don't worry." *Teacher takes child on her knee:* "There, is that better? Let's dry those tears." | 519 |
| 11. Warns child of danger *Teacher:* "Careful now, because we are near the road." *Teacher to child on swing:* "Debbie, careful; sit on properly." *Teacher:* "Mind, Katie, mind John! You might cut yourself on that spade." | 185 |
| 12. Suggests that child asks help from his mother *Teacher:* "Look, what's that?" (*pointing to a hole in a child's sock*) *Child:* "A hole." *Teacher:* "You'll have to ask your mummy to darn it." | 4 |
| 13. Grants immediately the child's request for help, objects, attention, or permission *Child, (holding up a nurse's apron):* "Will you do this up for me?" *Teacher, ties apron:* "Playing nurses, are you?" *Child:* "May I have a cloth to wipe up this milk?" *Teacher:* "Yes, of course, here it is." | 535 |
| 14. Shows admiration for, or interest in, a child's clothes, possessions, productions, or confidence in a child's relations, ideas, or interest in his home life *Teacher:* "Did you take your Daddy round the nursery?" *Teacher:* "What a pretty jumper! Is it a new one?" *Child:* "The doctor is coming to see my Daddy." *Teacher:* "Yes, poor Daddy has tonsilitis and is in bed; Mummy told me." | 533 |
| 15. Shares child's feelings and imaginative play, laughter, talks, or jokes Child pretends that it is after dinner. *Teacher:* "Yes, I see darling, so it's afternoon now." *Teacher:* "Tommy's come back, hasn't he? That's nice for you isn't it? I am glad." *Teacher, being led away to prison:* "I might try to escape." *Child:* "You're all tied up, you can't get away." | 361 |
| 16. Greets or draws child into a social situation *Teacher:* "Good morning Paul, hello Tom." *Teacher:* "Mary, would you like to see Paula's new book and her birthday cards? Perhaps you could both look at them." | 207 |

*TABLE 4 – Continued*

| Description | Total number of contacts from the 18 teachers |
| --- | --- |
| 17.  Shows pleasure in child's presence or interest in his personal condition<br>*Teacher:* "Show your sore finger to nurse, John."<br>*Child:* "I wasn't well yesterday."<br>*Teacher:* "You weren't well, oh dear, but now you are better, eh? We haven't seen that nice face for such a long time." | |
| 18.  Unspoken friendly contacts<br>Teacher sits down and takes child on her lap watching other children playing.<br>As one would expect from good nursery school-teachers, the records abound in evidence of friendly, personal interest in the children which is also reflected in the way in which many of the contacts which come into other categories are made. | 7 |
| 19.  Asks or invites child's help or co-operation, or draws attention to child's ability to help himself<br>*Teacher:* "Nigel, try to keep the clay on the table, please."<br>*Teacher:* "Would you like to throw that envelope away for me?" | 773 |
| 20.  Contacts likely to promote a good social attitude or an increase in social awareness by any of the following means:<br>    Recognizing or promoting co-operation.<br>    Suggesting that one child offers or gives, asks or accepts help from another.<br>    Suggesting that one child invites another to play with him.<br>    Pointing out the discomforts of one child to another.<br>    Reminding children that others have feelings.<br>*Teacher:* "Don't sit on his legs, darling, I'm sure you'll hurt him."<br>*Child:* "Bobby won't let me go upstairs."<br>*Teacher:* "Perhaps you haven't asked him nicely. It's very important how you ask. Go and ask Bobby nicely."<br>*Teacher:* "Stephen, this is rather too heavy to carry on your own. Help him, John."<br>*Children:* "We don't want Tommy."<br>*Teacher:* "Why not? I'm sure he will be very helpful in your play." | 695 |
| 21.  Demands a child's help or co-operation.<br>*Teacher:* "Ronnie, go and hang up your coat." | 178 |
| 22.  Agrees to grant a child's requests for objects, help, or permission after postponement<br>*Child (doing a puzzle):* "Will you help me?"<br>*Teacher:* "Yes, in a minute."<br>It is perhaps not self-evident why this contact should be | 149 |

*TABLE 4 – Continued*

| Description | Total number of contacts from the 18 teachers |
|---|---|
| placed in this group, but it is certainly one of the ways in which young children learn that the teacher has to be shared because of the needs of other children and therefore become aware that they can share here without losing her interest and help. | |
| 23. Thanks a child for help or gift (this is generally expressed simply as "Thank you Sam, etc.") *Teacher (taking a sweet):* "Oh, lovely, thank you." | 145 |
| 24. Arbitrates in a dispute *Teacher:* "Mary, you've had the pram a long time. Will you let Linda have a turn now?" *Teacher (as twins squeal):* "Kathleen, Kathleen! They belong to Margaret. You are a pair aren't you? | 123 |
| 25. Refuses child's help, gift, or production Child comes to teacher with a jar of water. *Teacher:* "Did you think I wanted it? We've nothing to put in it." Perhaps an explanation is needed here. This contact at first sight appears to be a discouragement rather than a promotion of social attitudes, but when the child's intention to help is recognized, as in the above example, he does not feel rebuffed but is often assisted in learning to help appropriately. | 39 |
| 26. Accepts the child's help or gifts *Child:* "It's for you!" (*showing a picture he has painted*). *Teacher:* "For me? Oh, but don't you want it for Mummy?" *Child:* "No, you can take it home." *Teacher:* "Oh, thank you! Would you like to tell me about your picture?" | 37 |
| 27. Apologies to child This contact (and No. 23) would be classified as II(c), since it is concerned with promoting good social attitudes by example. It is given here in order to preserve the sequence of contacts. *Teacher (knocking against child's house):* "Sorry, Bill, I trod on the back." | 34 |
| 28. Ask child's permission (this, too, is a II(c) contact) *Teacher (to a child who has just finished drawing):* "May I see your picture?" The chief features that emerge from this section is abundant evidence of the warmth and friendliness of the teachers and of their unhesitating readiness to give children full opportunity and encouragement to show in their turn friendly and helpful behaviour towards the teacher and to each other. | 1 |
| 29. Accepts a child's information and ideas *Child:* "We have built a bridge all morning." *Teacher:* "That's a good idea." | 17 |

*TABLE 4 – Continued*

| Description | Total number of contacts from the 18 teachers |
|---|---|
| 30. Encourages the child by admiration or approval of an achievement or production<br>Child shows stencils to teacher.<br>*Teacher:* "These two are beautiful. Try some more."<br>*Child (doing up his coat):* "Look!"<br>*Teacher:* "You can do it up. That's a good boy."<br>*Teacher (to child using waste material):* "Yes, it's coming on nicely." | 334 |
| 31. Encourages by suggestion<br>*Teacher:* "Are you going to put these flowers in water, John?"<br>*Child (showing picture):* "Look!"<br>*Teacher:* "You could stick it in something if you like." | 281 |
| 32. Commends child's behaviour<br>*Child:* "Can I give a sweet to little Joyce?"<br>*Teacher:* "That is nice of you." | 132 |
| 33. Encouragement by reassurance<br>*Alice:* "I can't cut these wings for my bird properly."<br>*Phyllis:* "Neither can I."<br>*Teacher:* "Now, Alice and Phyllis, when I show you, you can. I'm just coming."<br>*Teacher:* "That's better now." | 110 |
| 34. Reminds child of routine activity<br>*Teacher:* "Have you been to the toilet? (Child shakes his head).* Well, toilet first, please, or else you'll want to go in the middle of dinner." | 441 |
| 35. Gives a child a specific order<br>*Teacher:* "Bill, come off the table." | 339 |
| 36. Reproaches child for behaviour, untidiness, or noise<br>*Teacher:* "Oh, Bobby, look at your legs! What have you been doing? You could do with a bath." | 229 |
| 37. Refuses or deflects child's request for help, objects, attention, or permission<br>*Child:* "Can I come now?"<br>*Teacher:* "No, dear, not just now. Doctor doesn't want to see you." | 146 |
| 38. Checks child's activity<br>*Teacher (taking a toy gun):* "We won't play with that now." | 20 |
| 39. Ignores child's remark or action<br>*Child:* "Look at me, Miss X" *(sticks a green paper shape on his nose).*<br>*Teacher turns to another child and says:* "Was it this book you wanted?" | 19 |
| 40. Rejects, suggests, or reminds child of an acceptable form of behaviour<br>*Child:* "I needn't have an apron on?" | 50 |

*TABLE 4 — Continued*

| Description | Total number of contacts from the 18 teachers |
|---|---|
| *Teacher:* "Yes, to keep your dungarees clean, or you might get paint on them." | |
| The points which emerge here are the unhesitating acceptance of these teachers of the role of leadership and their responsibility for guiding the child to good social behaviour and sensible attitudes towards work. | |
| It is also evident that they use positive approaches very much more than negative and make very little use of punishment. Reproofs, when used, are nearly always courteous and gentle and very often are accompanied by constructive advice. Encouragement and praise are much more frequently used as a stimulus than reproof or reproach. | |
| 41. Meditates aloud | 155 |
| *Teacher:* "Oh, I wonder where it can be?" (*A piece of puzzle is missing*). | |
| 42. Seeks adult co-operation, asks or gives information to adult. | 27 |
| *Teacher to helper:* "Will you go and get Jill quickly? Her leg is stuck." | |
| 43. Mentions child to adult in child's presence. | 18 |
| *Teacher to helper:* "That's Lindy's basket. Go and hang it on her peg." | |
| 44. Mentions child to adult in hearing of other children | 15 |
| *Teacher to helper:* "Willie's made London Airport." | |
| 45. Exclamations used by teacher | 10 |
| *Child:* "Her head's come off" (*referring to paper doll*). | |
| *Teacher:* "Oh, what a shame." | |

CHAPTER 4

# Qualities observed in the Teachers in the Nursery Schools

*There is always a certain risk in being alive, and if you are more
alive, there is more risk.*

(Ibsen)

Although 18 teachers are not a large number from which to draw conclusions, it is interesting to see the differences between them and how the varying categories of contacts were used by them. Teacher C, with the highest score of all the 18 teachers (Table 3), does appear to be the most mature and successful of all the individuals observed, and so perhaps it is pertinent to use her as an example to illustrate many of the qualities which were found. A high score of contacts is not, however, necessarily a criterion of excellence. Children can be overwhelmed with smothering love, fed with unsuitable and indigestible intellectual information, never left to play independently, and have demands made on them for acceptable behaviour, good manners, attention to routines, etc., which are in no way suitable to their age and development.

However, it is not only the high number of contacts made by teacher C that strike one. It is their quality and kind, and the general picture of her playroom and personality which emerges. She had a group of 30 children with an average attendance of 25 and she had no 2-year-olds in the group when these observations were made.

Teacher C gave the impression of being a thoroughly happy person: young (about 26), active, and lively, but not fussy. Her mood was stable and her attitude consistent to both children and adults, and always welcoming. She was smiling and cheerful and yet had an inner quality of quietness which allowed the children, as it were, to "blossom". She obviously felt that the development of good social attitudes and social awareness were important, and she had the highest score in this category of all 18 teachers. She also scored highly in categories showing a warm and

20

loving response and acceptance of the child, and a building up of his feelings of adequacy and confidence. There was a notable lack of "fuss" in this group. When teacher C gave her attention to a child or a group of children she gave it very fully and appeared at leisure to carry on a really long and satisfactorily completed conversation. Instances of disputes were rare in this group and tended to be settled in a positive way.

> *Example: Sarah and new Janet both wanted to play with the same thing in the Wendy house.*
> *Janet:* "Miss C, she won't let me."
> *C:* "Look, Sarah, this is Janet, and she wants to play too."
> *Sarah:* "I'm the mummy."
> *C:* "Sometimes there are two mummies in one house, one up and one downstairs, or, Janet, perhaps you can be an Auntie."

Any kind of rejection or refusal by teacher C was rare, and she had a way of "softening the blow" or saving the child's face which went far to help him.

> *Example: Andrew was spoiling the group's singing and teacher C asked him not to, but, she added, "Sing nicely, like you usually do."*

If a child had to wait a turn, teacher C suggested an alternative or gave hope to a child that he would soon have his desire.

> *Example: Maurice wanted to make a fifth at the clay table.*

> *C:* "No, we can only have four, Maurice, or else the clay goes on the floor. Would you like to look at books just here, and then when one of these children have finished you'll be able to come? Perhaps someone won't be very long."

So often teacher C's explanations put the social point of view, drawing attention to other people's feelings and showing consideration of their convenience or happiness. She also showed a genuine sharing of her feelings and ideas with those of the children, and she not only sympathized with them, joining in with their joy or sorrow, she also shared such of her own feelings as were capable of being understood by the children concerned.

*Example: The children across the room in the rocking boat were singing* Golden Slumbers. *Teacher C joined in and sang across to them.*

She also had an intuitive sensing of the needs of the group.

*Example: Rita, a 4-year-old, had had a small fire in her house the evening before. Throughout the period she was constantly approaching teacher C with information about the fire, and teacher C was very generous in giving Rita the attention she needed. She listened to lengthy accounts and introduced opportunities for Rita to tell others of her experiences, suggested that Rita paint a picture of her fire, and then wrote down the story of the picture at Rita's dictation.*

Teacher C also scored highly in the giving of intellectual information to the children, though she did not overwhelm them with unwanted material, and her score for No. 1 was not as high as teacher D. On the other hand, she scored highly in inviting spontaneous information and ideas from the child himself.

If teacher C with the highest score of contacts was perhaps the most mature and well-balanced of all the teachers observed, interesting differences of techniques and personality, which were often enriching to the children appeared in the observations of the other 17 teachers. One got the impression from one or two of the teachers that they envisaged the nursery school rather as a children's workshop, and much of their time was spent in supplying information, encouraging skills, or suggesting additions to children's productions. New words would be introduced to them. Bobby, aged 4, said something about a window and the teacher told him that "windows in boats are called portholes". Their attention would be drawn to new and interesting things around them; a musical box was put on the table when a group of children were drinking their milk and the teacher asked them to listen to the music.

Sometimes one felt the children were a little overwhelmed when words and suggestions were made that were unacceptable. One teacher, anxious perhaps, to lead a child to more creative efforts, said brightly as she looked at what he was doing with his clay: "That's a lovely handle on your cup. Are you going to make a saucer?" "No," said the child firmly, "it's a mug."

Play, too, can be over-directed and lose its spontaneity, and a teacher can artificially stimulate an activity which the children have outlived.

Good teachers learn to avoid these pitfalls, but in the process of developing the art of giving the right and not the wrong kind of stimulus, some mistakes are made at first. Sometimes one felt that a teacher was uncertain of her rôle and function, not knowing when to step in and when to stand back; and sometimes this meant that she concerned herself with the equipment and materials rather than with the children, feeling, perhaps, that this was safer. This sometimes resulted in over-concern for the general order and tidiness of the room. Children will certainly need to be reminded to put things away, wipe up spills, keep sand off the floor, wash their hands, etc., but to be constantly demanding a rather adult-orientated conception of neat, tidy play can be exhausting and unproductive to everybody. A teacher, too, can sometimes hurry a child on to an activity of some kind before he is ready, because he appears to be doing nothing. In point of fact the need "to stand and stare", to take something in in order to make it one's own, to escape for a moment into an inner fantasy world, away from everyone and everything, is a very necessary part of growth.

Some groups of children seem to need more actual physical attention than others, and one teacher on a new housing estate appeared at first sight to be over-fussy about her children's physical needs and minor hurts. They were, however, an unsettled and rather insecure group, and one gradually became aware that this particular teacher was giving, obviously with satisfaction, something of real value to these children. With some teachers it might have taken a slightly different form. This teacher, however, felt that this was the best contribution she could make to help them to develop feelings of security.

The skill required to anticipate children's needs is an important one, and some teachers possess this quality in very good measure. The child who is not getting the help and notice he feels is his right can sometimes draw attention to himself in an awkward and time-consuming way. Thus one teacher often tended to arrive too late to prevent disaster when a child had already spilt the paint or got himself wet through as if he had almost unconsciously forced her to come to his aid and notice him. These sort of incidents, if they continue to happen throughout the day, can be extremely wearing, and by the end of a morning or afternoon both children and teacher can be over-tired coping with accidents that could have been avoided.

One or two teachers seemed to feel that children should be left very much alone, to develop in their own way, and rarely gave guidance, made suggestions, or offered help. No child, of course, wants his play dominated by the adult, nor does he want to be constantly told what to do. To find himself directed into one sort of play for one period and a different sort of play at another is very frustrating indeed. We are well aware today that children need long spells of uninterrupted play of their own choosing. On the other hand, children cannot learn everything from each other, or by trying things out for themselves, and the adult's experience and knowledge should be available to them. Obviously the teacher must provide a rich, exciting, secure, and challenging environment suitable to the children's needs and also be ready with help, ideas, and information where it is needed.

No teacher consciously denied children help when they requested it; sometimes they had to wait, but this is inevitable with a group of children. At times one felt, however, with one or two teachers that they stood back and took too passive a rôle, leaving their children to manage as best they could when active interest, participation, a sharing of knowledge, or a suggested new approach would have been welcomed. One teacher who had a group of rather young children did appear to find that she got very little stimulation back from the group. She actually said she was nothing but a glorified nursemaid, and gave the impression of being somewhat bored. One can sympathize with her feelings, even if one does not agree with her general assumption. It does emphasize the fact, however, that mixed aged groups are much more satisfactory. They are more natural, better for the children, and certainly more provocative and inspiring for the teacher.

The fact that the teacher's personal maturity is so important a factor in her ability to satisfy her children's demands really needs no research to prove. On the other hand, it is of value, perhaps to be able to underline it. It is surprising how often the young, uncertain, immature, and insecure teacher — sometimes straight from college — is given the youngest group of children in the school. In the infants school it will be the reception class. We still find the young nursery helper or the untrained nursery assistant in nursery schools, day nurseries, and residential nurseries being given far too much responsibility and having to take major decisions when they have neither the maturity, knowledge, nor experience to do so. We pay lip service to the fact that the years under 5 are one of the most formative and vital periods in a child's whole life, and yet we often put younger children in the sole charge of adults or adolescents who know little about the deeper needs and problems of childhood and are still in the process of trying to cope with their own difficulties. It must be remembered that young children's emotions are very near the surface, and they show their feelings of aggression, hostility, jealousy, love, and hate, often very spontaneously and freely in their behaviour to those around them. This can arouse all sorts of anxieties in the immature adult, bringing to the surface and reminding them, as it were, of many of their own unresolved conflicts and anxieties.

It is not enough, of course, just to say that a teacher must be mature, though this point has been emphasized. Certain specific qualities will obviously be more important and necessary than others in providing for the rather special needs of very young children; and these particular qualities do emerge in the personalities of the teachers selected and observed. It is very obvious, for example, how necessary it is to be able to give and receive affection, to share and co-operate in the children's interests, pleasures, joys, and sorrows, and there are countless examples of this ability with all the teachers observed.

It was generally the less-able individual who gave the most orders. One teacher was very anxious that her children should be independent, a very commendable thing. She did, however, give her children too many specific orders. ("Mary, go and wipe your face and hands", "John, put the bricks away", etc.). A more positive approach was used by the more secure teachers who sought to gain their children's co-operation. If they wanted help or a simple routine carried out, they would encourage independence rather than demand it.

All the teachers were aware of the need to encourage children in contacts likely to promote good social attitudes and an increase in social awareness. They realized that children could not be hurried in their social development, but that they could be helped by example and guidance and by the general feeling of ease, acceptance, and working together in the nursery. It was not always a good idea, however, to give children the impression which sometimes occurred that one only did something kind and thoughtful to somebody else because it might mean that they, in return, would do something kind and thoughtful back. Thus, to say to a child, "Come here and hold this coat for Peter and help him and then he will hold your coat for you", was a somewhat negative social approach, though probably better than nothing.

A number of the teachers showed special interest and admiration for the children's homes; clothes their mothers had made, things their fathers did, or their brothers and sisters had done. This made a real link for the children between school and home. Teachers greeted parents warmly, making them feel they were part of the nursery school, and this was of real benefit to the children.

The playrooms and materials also reflected the personalities of the teachers, and their own special interests were also apparent. One teacher who was very keen on children's paintings had a delightful and vivid collection in her room, while another had a room alive with plants and growing things. Thus the children were helped and stimulated in an environment that was educational in its fullest sense.

CHAPTER 5

# Co-operation between the Nursery School and the Family

*And I saw in the turning so clearly a child's*
*Forgotten mornings, when he walked with his mother*
*Through the parables*
*Of sunlight*
*And the legends of the green chapels*
*And the twice told fields of infancy*
*That his tears burned my cheeks and his heart moved in mine.*
(Dylan Thomas, Poem in October)

The subject of parent—teacher co-operation, the rôle the staff plays, and the relationship that exists between the two is a very pertinent subject at the moment, particularly when parent participation in the education and care of their children is very much in the news.

The Playgroups Association (a voluntary organization which provides play facilities for young children) tend to use parents as part of the staff, sometimes in a voluntary capacity, at other times as paid help. Some parents, of course, are trained teachers bringing up their own families but not wishing to go back to a full-time job; others are just interested parents, that is mothers with young children of their own, many of whom may be willing to attend lectures or a short part-time course (perhaps 8—10 lectures) to train them to work with young children more adequately. Nursery schools, of course, as part of primary education demand trained teachers in charge of the children. But this does not mean that the parents are in any way pushed out, or left out, just because they are not used as part of the teaching staff.

This study was planned to show, by careful observations and discussions with teachers and parents, the rôle that the nursery schools can play, how parents are involved, and the quality of the relationship that exists between school and home. The results are shown in Tables 5—7 at the end of this chapter.

27

The study was planned and conducted in the following way:

1. By making general observations and so building up an overall picture of the relationship between home and school, looking for points, however small, which would be indicative of the attitude of the parents.
2. By giving questionnaires to (a) mothers and (b) nursery school staff in an attempt to gain specific answers to certain questions.
3. By asking about parent—teacher associations.

Ten typical nursery schools were selected, not all of them in the south. Five schools — A, B, C, D, and E — were studied in detail; five — 1, 2, 3, 4, and 5 — in less detail, so that a more general picture of the latter was obtained which added to the general information. Five half-days were spent in schools A—E (with visits to parents' meetings whenever possible). In schools 1—5 a little less time was spent. The schools were working a combined system of part-time and full-time education.

The observer was often in the schools when new children were being admitted, and therefore a number of mothers were around, and it was possible to see how new children were settled in. The observer was very anxious to establish friendly relations by chatting easily and casually about the children, and questions were only asked and opinions sought when the observer herself (who was a trained experienced nursery school head) had gained the confidence of both parents and staff.

The questionnaires were given to 40 mothers who were willing and anxious to co-operate, though they did not know the exact reasons for the study (i.e. staff—parent relationships) and thought it was simply an interest in the children which, of course, it also was. The questionnaires were given towards the end of the term, and as the observer had already talked with the mothers and filled in some of the answers herself, the combination of written and verbal comments proved particularly valuable. Parents and staff were assured there were no "right" or "wrong" answers.

There were two main questions in the observer's mind:

1. What do mothers think about nursery schools?
2. What are the needs of present-day mothers and how successful is the school in meeting these needs?

Linked with this were such points as:

Is it just a matter of convenience that parents send their children to nursery school, and how is it seen as something of real value to the child?

Do parents recognize the professionalism of teachers and do they resent the fact that the teachers often appear more successful with their children than they are?

The questionnaire contained the following points:

What were the reasons for wanting your child in nursery school?
Is he or she benefiting? If so, in what ways?
Is there any benefit for you personally?
Is this your first experience of nursery school?
Is it as you expected, or did you find the programme or the atmosphere different from what you expected?
Do you feel welcome in the nursery school?
Do you feel that the parents' evenings and the discussion groups are good things to have? In what ways are they valuable?
Would you like them more frequently, or less?
Have you any problems or worries in bringing up your children, for instance over health, feeding, sleeping, toilet training, temper tantrums, fears, behaviour problems, or any others?
If you had problems, whose advice would you ask; neighbours, doctor, clinic, relations, books?
Would you feel free to talk about them to anyone in the nursery school?

*TABLE 5. Results of questionnaire*

|  | Times mentioned |
|---|---|
| *Reasons given by the mothers for wanting their children in nursery school (the replies of 40 mothers to the questionnaire)* | |
| Companionship | 30 |
| Excessive timidity | 4 |
| Lack of playing space | 4 |
| Good preparation for school | 4 |
| Highly strung and over-dependent | 3 |
| Need to make wider relationships | 2 |
| Too large an age gap between child and others in the family | 2 |
| Depression of mother | 2 |

*TABLE 5 — Continued*

|  | Times mentioned |
|---|---|
| Necessity of mother to work | 2 |
| Encourages children to think for themselves | 1 |
| Parents separated | 1 |

*Benefits children were receiving from attending nursery school*

|  |  |
|---|---|
| Companionship (including toleration, co-operation, interest in others, sharing toys) | 23 |
| Leading a fuller life with new experience and skills | 12 |
| Child is livelier and happier | 9 |
| Improvement in sleeping and eating | 9 |
| Learning to talk nicely | 1 |
| Increased confidence and independence | 11 |

*Personal benefits gained by mothers*

|  |  |
|---|---|
| More time for themselves, i.e. for shopping, looking after the baby, housework, etc. | 10 |
| Time for leisure pursuits | 6 |
| Spend more time with the family | 5 |
| Able to rest more | 2 |
| Reassurance and contentment because child is happy | 9 |
| Less frustration | 4 |
| Able to take a job | 3 |
| Learning more about children | 2 |
| No benefit | 5 |

|  |  |
|---|---|
| Mothers with previous experience of nursery school | 10 |
| Mothers with none | 25 |
| Found the nursery school what they expected | 26 |
| Found the nursery school different | 14 |
| Mothers who felt welcomed | 39 |
| Mothers who felt fairly welcomed | 1 |

|  |  |
|---|---|
| PTA meetings not worth while | 2 |
| PTA meetings very worth while | 24 |
| Parents who would like more meetings | 12 |
| Parents satisfied with the number | 8 |
| No comment | 20 |

*Problems encountered by parents bringing up their children*

|  |  |
|---|---|
| Sleeping | 11 |
| Feeding | 11 |
| Toilet training | 8 |
| Fears | 8 |

*TABLE 5 — Continued*

|  | Times mentioned |
|---|---|
| Temper tantrums | 7 |
| Health | 6 |
| Behaviour problems | 4 |
| No problems | 6 |

*Mothers would seek advice from*

| | |
|---|---|
| Doctor | 24 |
| Clinic | 13 |
| Relations (particularly own mother) | 11 |
| Books | 11 |
| Friends | 4 |
| Professional persons | 2 |
| Neighbours | 1 |

*Mothers who would discuss problems with nursery school staff*

| | |
|---|---|
| Mothers who would do so under certain circumstances | 5 |
| Mothers who would not | 4 |

*TABLE 6. Ways in which a friendly relationship is established with the mothers*

*Result of questionnaire given to 30 head teachers*

Allowing mothers to stay with their children
Encouraging them to talk about their problems
Being friendly and interested in them as people
Concerned with their families
Warmly welcoming
Telling mother of child's achievements
Encouraging them to look round the nursery
Asking mothers to supply materials
Introducing new mothers to each other ·
Explaining the aims and activities of the nursery
Relaxed, friendly atmosphere
Greetings and friendliness outside the school
Listening when mothers talked about their problems

TABLE 7. *Contacts between school and parents (incorporating the teachers'*
*questionnaire)*

|  | School |  |  |  |  |
|---|---|---|---|---|---|
|  | A | B | C | D | E |
| Personal greeting by head when child is brought to school each day | X | X | – | X | – |
| A friendly, welcoming atmosphere which included conversation and personal interest from every member of staff | X | X | X | X | X |
| Informative, helpful notices displayed in school | X | X | X | X | – |
| An information sheet given to new mothers | X | – | – | – | – |
| The practice of settling new children gradually | X | X | X | X | X |
| A lending library for mothers with books on child rearing, etc. | X | – | – | X | – |
| A library for children which the mothers can use and help the child to choose a book to take home | X | – | – | – | – |
| Staff introducing new mothers to each other | X | X | X | – | – |
| Providing time and place in school where mothers can meet together regularly | – | X | – | – | – |
| A parent–teacher association with regular meetings | X | X | X | X | – |
| Parents help with fund-raising activities | X | X | X | – | – |
| Special times set aside for parents to meet the head and discuss their children | – | – | – | X | – |
| Discussion groups arranged between parents and staff | X | – | – | – | – |
| Outings arranged for staff, mothers, and children | X | – | X | – | – |
| Parents help regularly in practical ways in the school | X | X | X | – | – |
| Parents help with special, and therefore less frequent, jobs or projects | X | X | X | X | – |
| Parents provide material which can be used in the children's activities | X | X | X | X | X |

| Schools | No. of contacts out of a possible 17 |
|---|---|
| A | 15 |
| B | 11 |
| C | 10 |
| D | 9 |
| E | 3 |

CHAPTER 6

# The Factors contributing to a
# Good Home—School Relationship

*Let children that would fear the Lord*
*Hear what their teachers say;*
*With rev'rence meet their parent's word,*
*And with delight obey.*

(Watts, *Divine Songs,* 1824)

The factors contributing to a good home—school relationship were far more numerous than one might imagine. It was only by breaking down the situations in the different schools that one became aware of the possibilities for interaction between teachers and parents.

The most important single factor was certainly the constant daily contact parents and teachers had together, and almost every school scored in this respect. The regular exchange between mothers and staff created this "co-operative environment" and was the foundation upon which more obvious examples of co-operation were built. When this was lacking, other contacts were less successful. The main advantage was that this included everyone. No matter how much effort was made in arranging meetings and other functions, there were always a few parents who were not reached by these methods. Home commitments, evening jobs, inability to find a baby-sitter, even shyness, had been given at various times as a reason. Whatever was mentioned, the fact remained that in many schools those parents would be virtually unknown, whereas in the nursery school the daily informal greetings enabled all the teachers and parents to build up a relationship together.

This informality was also shown in the way mothers were free to move around the schools. They could see for themselves that the school was not hiding anything from them and any suspicions they might have entertained were soon dispelled.

The teachers in most of the schools were quick to take advantage of

33

these casual contacts, and would point out pieces of work done by the children or would recount some particular achievement. Some teachers, particularly those in schools A, B, and D, were very much aware of the importance of their work with the parents, though it was doubtful whether every teacher realized how vital her contribution was. Many of them appeared to work on an intuitive level — adapting to the parents' needs much as they did to the childrens'. All agreed that home—school co-operation was very desirable, but one felt that some teachers were not really quite sure of their rôle until it was brought to their notice and they had to try and define it in words and in a statement of their beliefs.

One fact emerged clearly. It was not enough for the school to have parent—teacher co-operation as its official policy. Every member of the staff had to carry it out consistently. The very fact of being asked about their attitudes to parents did not make them change but did encourage them to clarify their feelings and ideas.

The teachers who were aware of their rôle both towards adults and children were the ones who had the strongest convictions, principles, and practice of nursery education. They worked with a calmness and assurance which not only provided security for the children but also increased confidence among the mothers. Most teachers recognized that even trivial happenings could cause anxiety if not really understood, and there was a general willingness to explain the smallest details of nursery school routine in order to reassure mothers. Plans for resting or feeding arrangements were often mentioned in this respect.

Fund-raising activities were frequently mentioned as examples of home—school co-operation, and parents involved in money-raising projects were obviously affected by this. Apart from the financial benefit to the school, there was the fact that parents and staff worked together for a common aim and shared success, and were brought much closer together. Barriers were broken down and the two groups labelled "parents" and "teachers" merged to become a group of people each with his own contribution to offer. Parents whose interest was aroused on a purely practical level showed increasing participation in all aspects of school life as they began to realize the deeper implications of nursery school education.

As far as the question of parents' need for advice was concerned, the inquiry showed that in a sympathetic setting many problems were revealed. The need, basically, was for a good listener; someone genuinely interested and able to accept both the parents and the problems without judging. The most successful were the teachers who were able to wait for the parents to admit the real problem. Those who were too eager to give advice would probably never discover the basic need and would, in fact, be advising on what was only a surface problem. Most teachers were skilled in this aspect of their work, with certain exceptions.

It was interesting to see that in the matter of parents' active participation there was basically no difference between working and middle-class mothers. This came out particularly in schools A and D. It also suggests that nursery schools are likely to be much more successful in this matter than those schools dealing with older children.

All the schools gave assent to the belief that home–school co-operation was essential although the number of contacts between the schools did differ. School A had the highest number of contacts and its parent– teacher relationships was excellent in every respect. The staff's unanimity of agreement on the policy towards parents and their consistency in carrying it out were striking. They were particularly conscious of the advisory function of the nursery school, and were skilled in creating an atmosphere in which parents could relax and talk freely. The settling of new children was done with great sensitivity.

School B, which was not a state-supported school, laid a greater emphasis on fund-raising, but this gave the parents a strong sense of responsibility towards "their" school. Involvement of the whole family was a feature here, and fathers shared the day-to-day activities to a greater extent than in most schools. This school also seemed particularly good at fostering friendships between parents. As in school A, the staff were very conscious of their work with the parents, and were sensitive to their needs.

In school C there was perhaps a little less awareness of parents' problems. The head felt that most parents were confident. Here the emphasis was more on practical day-to-day co-operation, and there was an enthusiastic response from the mothers when asked to help with a petition for more nursery schools. There was good liaison between the nursery and the infant school to which many of the children went, and the mothers were always reassured and helped if they were anxious about their children's transfer.

Although in school D the number of contacts appeared less than, for example, in school A, the relationship between the parents and staff was very good. This was the only school where special times were set aside regularly for parents to discuss their children with the head teacher. Miss X felt a very definite responsibility towards the parents and made every effort to get to know them, and there was real personal involvement between staff and parents.

School E was a pleasant, welcoming place, but there was perhaps just the vague feeling that parents could create problems and therefore their too active participation might make for difficulties which could be avoided. There was also a lack of space, which did often make parents' activities more awkward.

Schools 1—5 were visited less frequently and so less can really be said about them.

In school 1 the head was comparatively new and was in the process of getting to know the parents, but there was a welcoming and accepting atmosphere.

School 2 was also a pleasant, friendly place, but one got the impression that there was no very great desire on the part of the staff to get to know the parents better and that their work was with the children.

School 3 showed that there was more scope for parent—teacher contacts than the head and staff had been aware of, and the very fact of being asked about this had suddenly opened their eyes to its possibilities. There was, however, a feeling of confidence among the parents in the school and its ability to help them if needed, and there was a warm and welcoming approach.

Schools 4 and 5 were a little disappointing in their staff—parent relationships. It was friendly, but rather superficial. School 5 felt the parents were not really interested and (perhaps discouraged by previous failures) they were tending to accept their lack of success and leave it at that.

In nursery school A the children and parents were warmly greeted as they came in, and such remarks were heard by the observer as:

"Hello Paula, you've got a new coat on, just the colour that suits you. Your mother has been busy with her dressmaking again." Paula skips off smiling down the passage and her mother follows, smiling too.

"Good morning, Mrs. L. Any more news of your husband in hospital?" Mrs. L. starts to talk about her husband and her own anxiety and worry about his illness. It is suggested she keeps the head teacher informed and if there is anything they can do she must let them know.

In all the exchanges, and there were many more with other parents, there was a relaxed, friendly atmosphere. The mothers came into the nursery school enthusiastically, laughing and talking together, greeting each other, and commenting on the doings of their children and family events. In the playrooms the same feeling prevailed. Parents were greeted in a welcoming, easy way by the teachers and assistants. On a typical morning one mother might be showing the latest photograph of her children; another would be helping her child to a beaker of milk; yet another would be discussing some arrangements for collecting her child; while a fourth would be sitting in the book corner reading to her child before going home. It was very obvious that the school was very much a part of their lives.

In school B there was a constant stream of parents and children. A summer fete was under way at one period. There was much talk and laughter about what to bring, what stalls there would be, who should help where. Mothers went into the playroom, commenting on the growing plants everywhere. One child dragged her mother into the Wendy house to look at a new tea-set. Another mother helped her child choose something to play with. Almost all the mothers spent some minutes in the school until their child was happily settled. There was the same warm, friendly, informality as in school A, and when parents came to fetch their children they often stayed quietly in the background, listening perhaps to a story that was being told.

In school C the head teacher was moving around, greeting parents and helping to put out equipment. The feeling in the school and playrooms was very friendly, but as many of the children were part-time and the period they were in nursery school was short, there was, perhaps, a need for them to make the most of their time and to get settled down happily to play as soon as possible. The mothers, too, had to get home and then back again before lunch.

Those children called for at lunch-time went off in a leisurely way after showing their mothers something they had made or finished — perhaps a painting they had started. The same procedure applied to the afternoon children when they were called for.

Nursery school D opened onto a busy road so the door had to be kept shut, but once inside there was no formality. The mothers took their children into the large playroom where the head teacher was available with the children who had already arrived. From her position she could see the door and the parents and children coming in, and so was ready to greet everyone. Most of the mothers stayed watching their children for a while. One was so interested she stayed for 20 minutes though her own child was off playing somewhere else. When needed, the head teacher was always ready to talk quietly away from the hubbub of the children if the parents needed her. She was very familiar with the families and knew her children and their parents very well.

In school E the children came in by a side door and went direct to their own playrooms, but the head teacher was always around, and she laughed and joked with the children and the mothers as she saw them. The children often came along specially when they had hung up their coats to bring some flowers, a sweet, or to ask that their own treasured possessions should be looked after and kept safely for them until home time.

Schools 1—5 were all in their own way welcoming. School 1 was full of interesting things in the playrooms — pets, flowers, children's paintings — and the mothers often wandered about looking at these things. Such remarks were heard such as: "Oh, I like that, fancy our Mary doing such a good picture", or "Look what John's made out of the old boxes I sent along." In school 2 the mothers before leaving gave their children their beaker of milk which was set out for them, then waited until their child was happily settled.

Schools 3, 4, and 5 were friendly and kind in their own way.

In school 3 the head had her own group of children to prepare for, but the mothers almost always called in on their way to see their children were happily settled. The playrooms were very small and did not lend themselves to the presence of many adults.

Schools 4 and 5 were brisk in their contacts and perhaps less ready to talk to the mothers about their children. They were kindly and ready to do what they thought necessary, but in school 5 there were one or two rather discontented and disgruntled mothers who seemed to lack the happy, easy, personalities of those seen in the other schools. This had affected the staff, who were feeling somewhat discouraged about the relationships they were able to make.

In summing up this material concerned with the co-operation between the nursery school and the parents it became abundantly clear that the staff of the nursery schools from the very beginning were able to understand and accept the mothers' feelings about their children. Teachers recognized the ambivalent attitude of a mother urging her child towards independence and yet at the same time wanting to hold on to his babyhood. The mothers, in learning about and watching their own and other peoples' children by informal talk and seeing the teacher's approach, gained a deeper understanding of their own child and the stages he went through. The fact of having a break from their children enabled them to enjoy and manage them more easily and with less strain. The companionship of other mothers offered opportunities for widening the somewhat restricted lives some mothers with young children led. In building up good relationships many mothers found personal fulfilment and felt wanted and understood.

What future developments are there in the field of staff–parent relationships and is there anything more that can be done? Certain suggestions (some of which have already been tried) were considered as a result of this study, and the observations and discussions that took place between the observer, the mothers, and the staff.

What helps the mother helps the child, and vice versa, and whatever can be done to make mothers feel less lonely and isolated, cut off perhaps in large tower blocks of flats with often a very changing population, and to feel they are members of a kind and friendly community, is extremely valuable. If, when building schools of any kind, there could be a room put aside for parents where they could meet, chat, or do jobs for the school and the community, this would be extremely helpful. Many nursery schools are cramped for space, and every bit is needed for the children's lively activities, or a place for a quiet story time. Rooms are often either far too small to contain the children, the staff, and several mothers, or else they are in short supply.

There is a good deal of discussion (and differences of opinion too) as to whether parents, and mothers in particular should be used as auxiliary helpers in the playrooms under the direction of the teachers. The Playgroups Association does emphasize this particular activity, though it sounds very much easier in theory than it is in actual practice. Not every mother has the time to give; she may have other young children to care for, a husband on shift or night work, illness, etc., and one does not want these mothers to feel left out because they cannot offer to help although they would like to. Not every mother is suitable, and the fact of having a child of your own does not necessarily make you good with other peoples' children. Some mothers have very little idea of how to cope with children; they may be slow, inadequate, awkward, find making relationships difficult. They could in fact be really using the nursery children to work out all their own feelings of hostility, hate, jealousy, etc., which the children arouse in them. This might be helpful to them but could make the teacher's job extremely difficult. There are, of course, the helpful and efficient mothers who might be welcomed, but if these are the only ones who are always used as auxiliary helpers will they appear as favourites and so cause feelings of resentment among the other less-mature mothers?

How often, in a large nursery school, should individual mothers come in? Will they be paid, and are the children going to find it difficult to cope with a number of new people arriving to help? In a small community mothers naturally talk, and it is only too easy for Mrs. R, coming in as an auxiliary helper, to pass quite unintentionally comments about Mrs. Y's little boy who is aggressive, destructive, and uses bad language. Obviously the mothers would try to take on the attitude and approach of the trained teacher and also be helped to do so, but this takes time and skill on the part of both mothers and teachers.

Some children find it very difficult to share their mothers with other children and become aggressive, clinging, or weepy. Nor is it always easy for a mother to stand back and leave her child to fend for himself when, perhaps, she suddenly sees him on a piece of outdoor equipment and she thinks he will fall, or if he behaves in a very hostile way towards other children, "showing her up", as it were. To do nothing needs a lot of self-control. Certainly one would not dream of condemning the auxiliary help of mothers out of hand; it may work very well in some schools if they have specific jobs but much less well in others.

Mothers can, of course, give invaluable help, particularly in times of stress or when staff are away. This help need not necessarily, however, be in the playrooms with the children, but perhaps in the head teacher's room answering the telephone, taking messages, welcoming visitors, etc., in fact, in doing some of the hundred and one little jobs which do take up so much valuable time but which can be done very usefully by helpful mothers.

If a small group of children are taken out on a visit, extra help is always needed, and other needs of this kind can easily arise. These jobs are all linked with the children, yet are not really part of the teaching contacts in the classroom situation where trained adults are desirable. It is possible, of course, to have a therapeutic situation whereby in a very small group of children in charge of a highly skilled teacher or therapist, disturbed, inadequate, mothers can see, help, and discuss the way in which their own difficult children are acting out and working through unhappy family relationships in the play situation; but this is completely different from the normal nursery school which is not there to treat problem parents and children together in quite this way.

Many children coming to nursery school, even the younger ones, do feel that the world of home and school are separate. They impinge on each other and they work in harmony, but each has its own special identity and its own job to do. Whatever happens, however, the friendly co-operation and warm feelings which were so apparent in all the nursery schools in this study when parents felt free to come in and watch, take their time, settle their own child if necessary, talk with each other and the staff before going home, must not be jeopardized or lost in any way.

Another point that was made was that probably much more could be made of parents' backgrounds, especially fathers. They could be encouraged to call at the school in their uniforms of policeman, bus driver, fireman, etc. The children would admire the uniform and love to talk to them as they always find this a thrill. Small boys, too, long to identify with a man's world, and may have little idea of what their own father does. Maybe they can persuade their father to come along, even if he only has a rather boring brief case, but something can even be made of that.

Many parents, too, because of the particular work they do, can provide the nursery school with all sorts of waste material, which is always valuable.

Obviously all teachers in training should be made aware of the importance of the family and the relationship between the home and the school, though how teachers eventually manage the situation will depend very much on their maturity as individuals.

CHAPTER 7

# The Handicapped Child

*Happiness is like the relief from pain.*
(Grahame Greene)

What is the rôle of the teacher in relation to the handicapped child in the nursery school? Handicapped children tend to be isolated in their own homes and they need a great deal of individual help and understanding from their parents. Often they cannot join freely in the play of other children or make normal relationships. If their mothers take them out to the park or the shops they often feel anxious and unhappy because their child is so different from the other children they see around. From birth mutual communication and a two-way response is essential to healthy development, but natural handling by a mother will probably not produce a normal response from her child because of his particular handicap.

Obviously the child's attitude to the outside world, his feelings about himself, and the progress he is able to make will depend very much on how his parents react and feel about him and how far they are able to accept the fact that he is not, and never will be, quite like other children. It becomes particularly difficult as the child gets older. As a small baby his handicap may not seem very noticeable, but as he reaches the stage when he should be running about, talking, eager and responsive to everything, and is perhaps apathetic, helpless, unable to communicate, very slow in his reactions to his surroundings and other human beings, parents can find life very difficult and depressing.

What, too, is going to happen when such a child reaches compulsory school age. Will he, for example, have to be sent to a residential establishment?

In spite of the extra help parents often receive from the health department, the health visitor, the child guidance clinic, the handicapped child still has the same needs, feelings, and problems as that of the normal child. He wants love, security, understanding, and provision for purposeful play with other children around. This last he cannot always get in his own home. Therefore such children need the nursery school and the care of the trained teacher just as much as the normal child.

In this particular study among its 15 handicapped children observed

*TABLE 8. Handicapped children observed*

| School | Child | Handicap | Age at time of study |
|--------|-------|----------|----------------------|
| I | A | Meningitis, speech defect | 4.4 / 4.10 |
| | B | Fits, speech defect, etc. | 4.6 / 4.10 |
| | C | Epileptic, retarded | 5.11 / 6.4 |
| II | D | Congenital defects of eyes and thumbs | 4.4 / 4.9 |
| | E | Non-communicator | 4.2 / 4.7 |
| | F | Mongol | 4.3 / 4.5 |
| III | G | Aphasic | 4.2 / 4.3 |
| | H | Spastic, retarded | 5.7 / 6.0 |
| | I | Obese, retarded | 3.8 / 4.1 |
| | J | Slightly spastic | 4.3 / 4.9 |
| IV | K | Spastic | 4.9 / 5.2 |
| | L | Speech and hearing defect | 4.7 / 4.11 |
| V | M | Retarded speech and visual defects | 4.5 / 4.11 |
| | N | Mongol | 3.5 / 3.11 |
| | O | Speech defect. Very disturbed | 4.8 / 5.0 |

were 6 who through meningitis, epilepsy, and mongolism were subnormal in their development, and 4 with varying degrees of handicap through lack of ability to communicate. They were observed in 5 different nursery schools from a fairly wide area (6 areas were examined). Twelve nursery schools were originally approached and 5 were finally selected. All the nursery schools were working with full- and part-time groups of children. All were well equipped and adequately staffed, and catered for children from a variety of different backgrounds. Time samples of the 15 children were taken at 2 different periods in the year. (See Table 8.)

Obviously one of the problems that teachers have to face when they have very disturbed or handicapped children in the group is the amount of time and attention they are going to take. Will they need the speech therapist to visit them in nursery school or someone to give them special exercises? Do they use aids of some kind? (Normal children are often very interested in other children's glasses, deaf aids, etc., and often want to handle them). Will they have to be very carefully watched on, perhaps, the outdoor equipment? Will they interfere seriously with the activities and play of the other children in the group? A very disturbed child can be so unpredictable that he needs constant watching in case he harms himself or someone else.

The environment of the nursery school is not really geared to cope with the child with serious disabilities, yet such children often need a secure and challenging setting with other children around very badly.

Obviously the number accepted in a group will depend on the amount of help they need and the quality of the staff, as at certain periods of the day they may be extremely time-consuming.

The teacher's rôle is extremely important as the parents themselves will need all the support and reassurance that it is possible to give them.

The child may need a long period with his mother near at hand during his settling-in period, while at the same time his mother may need a good deal of help in allowing her child to be as independent as possible as the temptation is often to over-protect him.

Every achievement on the part of the child is vital and must be encouraged and praised and pointed out to his mother as he will have to exert himself a great deal more than the normal boy or girl to achieve far less, and will become very discouraged and frustrated if there is, for example, no adult near at hand when he needs one.

The potential for learning is inherent in every child, but to continue to want to learn a boy or girl needs to be provided with materials which are exciting and challenging but which the nursery school staff know can eventually be productive; for nothing succeeds like success, while continual failure is heart-breaking to any child.

In normal development there is a steady progression through the sensory, motor, perceptual, language, and conceptual levels, but the child with a disability is always later in certain developmental stages, and yet no stage can be missed without ill effects. Close co-operation is needed with outside agencies as everyone needs to know what is involved in a particular handicap. Part of the understanding skill of the staff lies in their ability to see the child in a quite unsentimental way, considering his problems realistically yet at the same time giving him the love and support he must have. Another task of the staff is often to plan and adapt the equipment in an imaginative way to entice the child to use it.

Because the children in this study were each observed at two different periods a few months apart, it was possible to see by the summaries of their behaviour (examples given) the improvement they had made. Even though it was in no way particularly spectacular there was progress, and the children werè responding more positively.

By looking at Table 9 it is possible to see the kind of activities the children were taking part in, and Table 10 shows the average number of handicapped children in the different schools.

One must remember also that each of these children needed even more care and attention (often involving physical help) than the normal nursery school child. Teachers and assistants therefore had to be extremely alert, ready to step in, or stand back according to the particular situation or the handicap of an individual child yet in no way to neglect the normal children in the group. It involved a close and understanding relationship with the parents. This was no easy task, yet all the teachers concerned felt how important it was that these children were able to enjoy and benefit from attendance at a nursery school.

## C A S E S

### K (H A N D I C A P: S P A S T I C)

*January, 4 years 9 months*

She arrived in nursery school after physiotherapy and spent a lot of time on routine tasks. At any kind of creative play the adult had to give her a lot of very subtle help. There was very careful structuring of the nursery school physical apparatus before K went out. She wanted to use the outdoor equipment and she also enjoyed the music period. She was very immature emotionally and socially, and needed an adult to help her converse.

*June, 5 years 2 months*

K has had her leg in plaster again and has needed and received constant staff encouragement, from firmness to gentle laughter and joking, to help her to manage. The other children help her too, in her physical play, and K now often succeeds in what she wants to achieve stimulated by her peers. The outdoor equipment had not been specially structured on this occasion. There is definite improvement: she is more friendly even though demanding of help.

## M (HANDICAP: VERY RETARDED; SPEECH AND EYE DEFECTS)

*January, 4 years 6 months*

M displayed more periods of inactivity than any of the other handicapped children studied. He appeared to be 2 years behind in total development. He was very timid, though he did watch and listen to other children at play. He shared quite readily in group activities and managed finger plays at his own very slow rate; he clapped and laughed when he achieved this. Certain adults seemed very important to him. One of the staff told the observer that his play on this particular morning had progressed, as this was the first time she had seen him move away from her and pick up a truck for himself to play with.

*June, 4 years 11 months*

M's play was a little more varied. The other children were beginning to take notice of him in various ways and draw him into their play. The staff were trying very hard to interest and stimulate him and he was beginning to respond. He attempted to assert himself and showed some imagination in his play, but he was still very slow although beginning very gradually to react to the nursery school environment.

## I (HANDICAP: OBESE AND RETARDED)

*January, 3 years 8 months*

Very helpless, partly due to physical bulk but also to mother's indulgent attitude. The teacher had to persuade and guide her towards play materials. Much of her movements resembled those of a 2-year-old child. Her language usually consisted of obscene words or commands. She used the third person when talking about herself. Her play was repetitive; very slow in everything she did and very easily frustrated. She did not want to come to nursery school.

*June, 4 years 1 month*

She now wants to come to nursery school and seems to enjoy her play. Both her movements and appearance have improved, but she is still grossly fat and pale-faced, and needs adult help constantly. She shows persistence and a certain desire to experiment in her play, though it is still very obsessive. She is very spoilt and is still verbally aggressive and abusive, though she is trying to be friendly.

D (HANDICAP: CONGENITAL DEFECTS OF EYES AND HANDS)

*February, 4 years 4 months*

His play often consisted in periods of apathetic inactivity interspersed with activities somewhat disturbing to the group. He was erratic and unsettled and seemed more interested in people than things.

*July, 4 years 9 months*

Some of his former frustrations still apparent, but on the whole his aggression more easily resolved more normally in play situations. He seems now to use play materials for experiences in handling and controlling situations. He understands and reasons better, his play is more constructive, and his interest is sustained for longer periods. His deep fantasy play appears more balanced and normal. He shows possibilities of fitting into a normal infant school. He still often shows frustration when unsuccessful, but is much less demanding of help.

Parent involvement, i.e. the opportunity for mothers to watch their children in their play, can be reassuring, and voluntary help from either a mother or other interested adult can be extremely useful in helping a severely disabled child to play as he may need to be cared for on almost a one-to-one basis. The child's own mother is probably not the best person to do this. She has no doubt had her fill of her handicapped child and needs a rest from him. Whoever comes along to give extra help, it should be regular and consistent otherwise a child will be at the mercy of a constantly changing pattern of grown-ups, each one having to learn afresh the nature of the handicap and what the child can or cannot do.

It is a good thing that those children with no disability should learn from the children who have such problems, and that those who can do things for themselves should see what it is like to be helpless and inadequate. It is surprising how understanding young children can be and how ready they are to help those less fortunate than themselves.

Anyone who visits the nursery school can also see something of the difficulties of these children and the problems of those who care for them.

TABLE 9. Percentage of time spent on various activities

| | A | | B | | C | | D | | E | | F | | G | | H | |
|---|---|---|---|---|---|---|---|---|---|---|---|---|---|---|---|---|
| | 1 | 2 | 1 | 2 | 1 | 2 | 1 | 2 | 1 | 2 | 1 | 2 | 1 | 2 | 1 | 2 |
| Activity (solitary but purposeful) | 2·2 | | | | 13·9 | ·5 | 1·6 | | 1·6 | | 4·4 | | 3·8 | | 5·5 | 2 |
| Aggression, disturbed activity | | 1·6 | | | 9·4 | 8·8 | | 8·3 | | | | 1·6 | | | | |
| Animals | | 16·6 | | | | ·5 | | | | | | 6·6 | 2·8 | | ·5 | |
| Apparatus (large, physical) | 22 | 16·6 | | | | | | | | | 27·8 | 8·3 | | | 5 | |
| Apparent inactivity | 22 | 10 | 15·5 | 13·3 | 18·3 | | 27·8 | | 27·8 | | 8·3 | | 13·9 | 16·6 | 16·6 | 16·6 |
| Books | | | | | | | | | 2·8 | | | | | | | |
| Blocks | | | | | | | | | | | 1·6 | | | | | |
| Clay & plasticine | | | | | | | | | | | 1·0 | | | | | |
| Clearing away | | | | | | | | | | | 5 | | | | | |
| Creative | | | | | | | | | | | | | | | 5·5 | |
| Discovery, experimental | 11·1 | 20 | 1·1 | 13·3 | 11·1 | 5 | | | 16·6 | | 11·1 | 8·3 | 2·2 | 25 | | |
| Dough, pastry | | 6·6 | | | 2·7 | | 16·6 | | | | | | | 25 | | |
| Dressing up | 1·1 | 17·7 | | | 3·5 | | | | | | | 33·3 | | | | |
| Imaginative play | | | | | 19·4 | 16·6 | | 25 | 20 | | 2·8 | | | | | |
| Large construction planks, boxes, tyres | | | | | 16·6 | 48·3 | | 41·6 | | | | | 13·9 | 33·3 | | |
| Music | 2·8 | 16·6 | | | 11·1 | 16·6 | 2·8 | 30 | | | | | | | 5·5 | 46·6 |
| Painting | 2·8 | 1·6 | | | 5·5 | | 27·8 | 25 | | | 1·6 | | | | | |
| Puzzles, table occupations | 32·2 | | | 73·3 | 13·3 | | 5 | | 5 | | | 33·3 | | 33·3 | | |
| Routine | 1·1 | 4·5 | | | 5·5 | | 7·2 | | | | 5·5 | | 5·5 | 13·8 | 11·1 | |
| Sand (dry) | 3·3 | 6·6 | | | 30·5 | | | | | | ·5 | | | | 19·4 | 16·6 |
| Sand (wet) | | | | | 1·1 | | | 3·3 | | | | | | | 8·3 | 3·3 |
| Story & group times | | | | | 2·8 | | | | | | 2·8 | 8·3 | 8·3 | | 5·5 | |
| Water | | | | | | | | | 8·3 | 8·3 | | | | | | |
| Wendy house; doll play | | | | | | | | | | | | | | | | 26·6 |
| Time not used | 33 | | 33 | | | | | | | | | | 25 | | | |

TABLE 9 – Continued

| | I | | J | | K | | L | | M | | N | | O | |
|---|---|---|---|---|---|---|---|---|---|---|---|---|---|---|
| | 1 | 2 | 1 | 2 | 1 | 2 | 1 | 2 | 1 | 2 | 1 | 2 | 1 | 2 |
| Activity (solitary but purposeful) | 5·5 | | | | 5·5 | | 5·5 | | 5·5 | 8·3 | | | 5·5 | 20 |
| Aggression, disturbed activity | 8·3 | | 2·8 | | | | 11·1 | | | | | 8·3 | | 5 |
| Animals | | | 5 | 5 | 1·6 | | | | | | | | | |
| Apparatus (large, physical) | 5·5 | | 5·5 | 33·3 | 42·2 | 66·6 | | 20 | 19·4 | 30 | 5·5 | 20 | | 25 |
| Apparent inactivity | 5·5 | | | | 8·3 | | | | 38·8 | 38·3 | 5·5 | | 15 | 8·3 |
| Books | | | | | | | 16·6 | 8·3 | | | 10·5 | | | |
| Blocks | 36·1 | | | | | | | | | | 3·3 | | | |
| Clay & plasticine | 2·8 | | | | | | | | | | 2·2 | | | |
| Clearing away | | | | | | | | | | | | | | |
| Creative | | | 20 | | 5·5 | | 13·9 | | | | 4·4 | | 6·6 | |
| Discovery, experimental | | | | | 13·9 | | | | | 8·3 | 6·6 | 25 | | |
| Dough, pastry | | | | | | | | | | | 2·8 | | | |
| Dressing up | | | | | | | | | | | 3·3 | | | |
| Imaginative play | | | | | 16·6 | | 16·6 | | | | 2·8 | | | |
| Large construction planks, boxes, tyres | | | | 31·6 | 6·6 | 8·3 | | | | 6·6 | | | | |
| Music | 5·5 | 16·6 | 5·5 | | | | | | | | | | | |
| Painting | 11·1 | | | | | | | | | | 1·6 | 30 | 13·3 | 41·6 |
| Puzzles, table occupations | 8·3 | | | | 30 | 21·6 | 22·2 | 41·6 | | | 10·5 | | 11·1 | |
| Routine | 8·3 | | 5·5 | 5 | | | | 13·3 | 5·5 | | 12·2 | | 6·6 | |
| Sand (dry) | | | 19·4 | | | | | | | | 8·3 | | | |
| Sand (wet) | | | 11·1 | | | 3·3 | | 16·6 | | | | | | |
| Story & group times | 8·3 | | 11·1 | | | | | | 13·9 | 8·3 | 11·1 | | | |
| Water | 25 | 30 | 27·8 | | 5·5 | 8·3 | 8·3 | | 16·6 | | 8·3 | | 25 | |
| Wendy house; doll play | | | | | | | | | | | | 16·6 | 5·5 | |
| Time not used | | | 16·6 | | | | | | | | | | 11·1 | |

TABLE 10. Results of questionnaires to show numbers of handicapped children in nursery schools, with categories of handicap

|  | Area* | | | | | |
|---|---|---|---|---|---|---|
|  | A | B | C | D | E | F |
| No. of schools in area | 4 | 12 | 10 | 17 | 6 | 6 |
| Total no. of nursery children on roll in area | 280 | 1008 | 682 | 1690 | 362 | 363 |
| Average no. of children in each school | 70 | 84 | 68 | 99 | 60 | 60 |
| No. of handicapped children at nursery schools in area | 17+(see notes) | 80 | 74 | 68 | 57 | 26 |
| Average no. of handicapped children per school | 4+ | 7 | 7+ | 4 | 9+ | 4 |
| Usual no. on roll (proportion) | Variable to 10% | Variable, 2 per group No record or 10% | Variable, 1 per group up to 10% | None to 10% | Variable, 2 per group to 25% | Variable to 7% |
| **Categories** | | | | | | |
| Spastic | 1 | 2 | 4 | 4 | 1 | — |
| Congenital deformity | 1 | 3+1 | 2 | — | 3 | 1 |
| Heart | 4 | 4 | 1 | 1 | 3 | 1 |
| Hydrocephalus | — | — | 1 | — | — | — |
| Obese | — | — | 1 | — | — | — |
| Partially blind | — | 2 | 1 | 2 | — | — |
| Epileptic | — | 2 | 1 | 2 | — | — |
| Mentally handicapped | 4 | 6 | 7 | 7 | 6 | 5 |
| Mongol | 1 | 1 | 2 | 1 | — | — |
| Autistic | — | — | 1 | — | — | — |
| Backward in speech and non-communicators | 3+2 | 37+8 | 28+6 | 34+13 | 25+3 | 14 |

*TABLE 10 – Continued*

|  |  |  |  |  |  |
|---|---|---|---|---|---|
| Deaf | — | — | 1 | 2 | — |
| Partially deaf | 3 | 1 | 4 | 2 | 5 |
| Disturbed or maladjusted | 2 | 12 | 18 | 11 | 24 |
| Thyroid, asthma, malnutrition, etc. | 1 | 1 | — | 3 | 1 |
| Recommendations |  |  |  |  |  |
| MOH | 7 | 35 | 41 | 9 | 15 |
| Child guidance | 1 | 8 | 4 | 2 | 9 |
| Health visitor | 4 | 29 | 13 | 5 | 21 |
| GP | — | 11 | 5 | 1 | 3 |
| Pediatrician | 2 | 2 | ++ | 4 | — |
| Children's department | 1 | 2 | — | — | — |
| Audiology speech clinic | — | 8 | 1 | — | — |
| Mother and medical | 1 | 5 | — | 10 | — |
| Waiting list | 1 | 21 | 41 | 21 | 11 |

TABLE 11. *Comments on results of questionnaires*

| Area | Special services | Other points of interest |
|---|---|---|
| A | 1. Help from managers alongside medical and other services.<br>2. System of co-operation between some nursery schools and adjoining primary school. Handicapped child attends each for some part of a day.<br>3. Extra assistant allowed readily for school where boy needed ratio "one to one". | 1. Need mentioned by more than one head to get more co-operation with parents and families of their handicapped children.<br>2. New school opened this year when old prefabricated building demolished. Two classes and staff transferred to new building. Children helped with the "move" Additional class in new building is for 10 severely handicapped children who mix with other children for parts of day. Teacher in charge of group from a hospital. |
| B<br>. | 1. Good services and help to most of the schools.<br>2. Monthly "community" meetings in form of luncheon. Head teachers, GPs, MOH, Child Guidance and Children's Department, and Magistrates meet and discuss common problems.<br>3. Many special schools locally for most handicaps except for blind whose provision is residential.<br>4. Delayed speech unit within one nursery school. | 1. Many of handicaps, which could eventually have delayed learning, only discovered after nursery school admission – from ordinary list.<br>2. One school caters for 3–7-year-olds. Handicapped children need not therefore move at 5 years.<br>3. Head gave comparative figures of her handicapped children last year. |
| C<br>q<br><br>q | 1. Good co-operation with various departments and services in most districts.<br>2. Special services department will give advice re admissions to nursery schools.<br>3. Medical, child guidance, and pediatrician work closely in most districts.<br>4. Teachers of the deaf give valuable help in area. | 1. Eye defects and 2 deaf children discovered after nursery admission at school examination.<br>2. Some heads commented that many children now are already entered on the waiting list personally, by parent, before department have suggested nursery school. |
| D | 1. One head says district well served by spastic, deaf, and mentally handicapped schools.<br>2. Second head comments on physically handicapped school provision and on that for the deaf. | 1. Five schools with large numbers on roll claim to have no handicapped children in attendance (note speech and communication section as compared with A, B, C, E, and F). |

| Area | Special services | Other points of interest |
|---|---|---|
| | 3. No other comments on help from services at the other 15 schools. | 2. One school claims to have had no handicapped children for 3 years.<br>3. Two mention system in their area of new link with schools for the deaf. |
| E | 1. Good co-operation apparent with health visitors and medical department.<br>2. Good co-operation apparent with hospital Audiology Unit.<br>3. Assessment unit mentioned for nursery-aged children in special school. | 1. Medical examination before child enters nursery. |
| F | No mention of medical or other services helping. | Two deaf children not discovered until medical examination.. |

CHAPTER 8

# Relationships with the Nursery Assistant

*I can give you the explanation Ma'am but not the understanding of it.*

(Dr. Johnson)

The rôle of the teacher in relation to her nursery assistant who has obtained her NNEB certificate is not always an easy one to manage successfully. It might, therefore, be useful to see what is involved in the training a nursery assistant receives and how it relates to that of the teacher.*

The training covers a 2-year course for girls of 16 years of age and also for older women, though there are shorter courses in some cases for persons with special qualifications and experience. There are no absolute first qualifications demanded. Applicants have a personal interview, but some colleges of further education do require two or more GCE or CSE grade I passes. It is usual to spend one-third of the course at the college and two-thirds working with the children. There is an examination at the end of the course and a certificate is awarded. It must be remembered, however, that this is not a teacher-training and the nursery assistant is not a qualified teacher who has had a college training and has obtained her teacher's certificate.

The trained teacher, therefore, has the overall responsibility of the children, the organization, the planning of the day routines, policy making, and the layout of the playroom; the assistant is there to help her.

Naturally the teacher is deeply concerned with the children's all-round development, and it is extremely important that the teacher and her assistant work harmoniously together so that the children get the maximum benefit from their time at the nursery school. There are always a great many routine jobs to do at the beginning of the nursery school day

---

*The NNEB training is going through certain new stages and is in a somewhat fluid state.

54

such as preparing the playroom and the materials and attending to the general attractiveness of the room. As a rule the teacher and the assistant do these tasks together. One does not want the assistant to feel she is always the person who has to do all the odd jobs, and obviously the teacher will want her assistant to know that she is prepared to take her share of the less exciting things and that she is not asking her assistant to do something she herself either cannot do or is not prepared to do.

A very important task, as far as the child is concerned, is dealing with a boy or girl who has been sick or wet or soiled himself. At such times a child will be very worried, frightened, and anxious, and the situation needs to be handled by a loving and familiar adult. (Personally, I [the author] always undertook these jobs myself if I possibly could. I knew the children, all of them, and I wanted my staff to realize that anything and everything connected with a child's comfort and wellbeing is important, and this particular task extremely so.)

Often, of course, the assistant will have to deal with this sort of accident as the teacher has the rest of her group of children to care for, and the head may be busy. However, it is very important that the assistant does not think she is always expected to do what some may consider the dirty, objectionable chores, which the teacher is not prepared to tackle. It can sometimes help things and prove most instructive to both if the teacher and her assistant change places and each does the other's work.

Frank discussion between the teacher and her assistant always pays dividends. Both share in what is planned, and the assistant feels free to make suggestions and ask questions. A few minutes discussing individual children at the end of the day is very helpful, as the assistant may have had a longer and more productive relationship with a certain child than the teacher. There should, too, be a common policy for dealing with certain situations, i.e. behaviour problems, so that the children know what to expect and do not play one member of the staff off against another.

There are sometimes difficulties if the nursery assistant is older and more experienced than the trained teacher, especially if the latter is in her first job. The nursery assistant may be rather bossy and over-confident and know the parents and children better and over a longer period. She may be giving the wrong advice or have gossiped about matters which are confidential. If this continues to happen the head teacher may have to step in and support the teacher and in some cases move the assistant to another group of children if the difficulties cannot be resolved after a free and friendly discussion between them. Before taking any drastic measures of this kind, however, the nursery assistant can often be helped to understand how necessary her support and knowledge of the children and parents can be to the teacher; and the teacher herself should be prepared to benefit and learn from the longer experience of her assistant.

In the long run, however, the teacher is ultimately responsible, and she must organize the situation as she sees fit. The nursery assistant is never going to respect the teacher who cannot really take charge. Hard work is obviously necessary. The teacher who is always late, rushes off home at the first possible moment, and is lazy and ineffectual, will never get the respect she may feel is her due from her nursery assistant or the other staff.

If the nursery assistant is coping adequately with a situation (i.e. a child in difficulties or a parent discussing some problem) she should be left to finish it, and if she feels there are certain tasks she is responsible for, it will make her feel more a part of the group.

Any particular skill the nursery assistant possesses should be used to the full: she may play the piano or have "green fingers", she can then be a real asset to the group. Just as the playroom should be ready for the children in the morning, so when they go home things must be tidied away but not before the children have finished playing. (Sometimes the assistant is so anxious to get the equipment put away or to do some necessary cleaning that the children are left with nothing to play with at all.) The nursery assistant can take a story or music period if she can do this successfully. Her help with any records which are kept of the children's progress is also vital. She may see aspects of the child that the teacher has missed.

It is easy for both the teacher and the nursery assistant to get into a rut, and if it is possible to arrange visits to other nursery schools, exhibitions, lectures, etc., this can be a real inspiration for them both. If the nursery school is used by student teachers in training they, too, often bring new ideas into the nursery. The head teacher should also be ready with ideas such as the titles of new books; and she should keep her staff informed of any developments in the LEA's policy in regard to education as a whole and particularly if it affects the nursery schools.

The young student nursery assistant in training will obviously take her cue from the trained staff and the nursery assistant, and will imitate their behaviour. She, too, needs to feel part of the group and have her share in doing things such as playing and helping with the children rather than spending all her time washing or clearing up. There should be close co-operation between the training tutor and the nursery school staff, so that together they can see that the young nursery assistant in training gets the sort of experience with the children that she needs (perhaps telling a story or sharing in music time).

If there is a known and expected policy in the nursery school in regard to certain fundamental things, this will help all the staff concerned; the parents, too, will accept these ideals and values without question.

The teacher, therefore, whether as the head or in charge of a group of children with her assistant and young nursery helper in training, has this vital role to play — the making and keeping of good relationships within the school and group and this, of course, involves as has already been emphasized, caring for the all-round development of the children in her care. It will be her maturity and example which will make this possible.

CHAPTER 9

# Settling New Children into Nursery School

*They picked me up bodily, kicking and bawling and carried me up*
*the road.*
*"Boys who don't go to school get put into boxes, and turn into*
*rabbits and get chopped up Sundays",*
*I felt this was overdoing it rather, but I said no more after that.*

(Laurie Lee, Cider with Rosie)

The teacher has an important rôle to play in providing for the comfort and security of the children in her care, and this is particularly true when settling in new children who are just starting nursery school.

For a child to leave home, perhaps for the first time, and to venture into the large and often overwhelming world of school, even nursery school, can be a devastating experience. Home has its own precious and familiar landscape; it is small and intimate, and it is generally inhabited by the continual presence of "mother" even though she is involved in household tasks, is often busy, and at times harassed and impatient. She does, however, make the child's day. She feeds him, washes him, comforts him when he cries, and although there will be moments when, absorbed in his own play, he may almost forget she is there, when he suddenly needs her loving company she will be around somewhere not too far away. The nursery school environment, even with its child-size furniture and fittings, must often appear immense, the garden stretching away into a distance beyond knowing; playrooms, passages, cloakrooms, all full of incredibly noisy, active, and unknown children of all sorts and shapes and sizes.

Every child who comes to nursery school is an individual, a person in his own right with his own spontaneous personality. He brings with him all his past experiences whatever they may be. He may exude confidence and wellbeing, aggressive and destructive hostility, shy withdrawal, or timid anxiety.

58

It is not always easy for parents to decide to send their child to nursery school. They know its value but they know, too, that the house will lose some of its gaiety when the children are not there. The home, however, has not really enough to offer an active, lively child who has to be dragged round the shops, is into everything, is noisy and curious, and avid for the company of other children. The nursery school has so much to offer, yet the first break with home can be a frightening and anxious time for a child, and the way in which to make this new experience exciting, yet sufficiently secure to give him a feeling of independence without undue anxiety, is something which deeply concerns both parents and teachers.

It is important to "temper the wind to the shorn lamb" and to see that a child's first group contacts, his first eager or hesitant steps beyond his own threshold, are sufficiently satisfying ones to make their continuation worthwhile.

What are the ways in which the settling-in process can prove a happy one for both mother and child so that each can come to terms with this new and separate life?

Should mother, for example, hurry away almost at her child's first moment of entry into this new and strange world leaving him to manage, as best he can, to come to terms with the newness and the strangeness; to learn as quickly as possible, perhaps the hard way, to manage without her? It will, in any case, be little use to reassure him that she will be "back soon", for time has no meaning to the under-five and 20 minutes without mother can seem an eternity of desolation. Or is it better and less of a shock for a child to get accustomed to nursery school gradually, to stay for only a very short time on the first day, with mother with him in the  playroom? Then, as time passes, he can stay a little longer, left occasionally while mother goes shopping, but never entirely deserted until he seems ready and willing to be without her. Surely this is the way we would all want our children to begin school?

Many mothers quite naturally, even when their child has been at nursery school for some time, wait to see him happily settled at play. In reading of the relationship between teachers and parents it is very obvious how much they enjoyed their morning and afternoon contacts and how much, too, they felt they were really a part of the nursery school.

Just occasionally a mother may try to cling unduly to her child. He is really longing to be left to his own devices, yet she cannot bear to relinquish him. Sometimes the child himself feels guilty if he does not, as it were, cling to his mother and cry to show her he still loves and needs her. Then the help of the skilled teacher may be required to end this loving but demanding tug-of-war, so that neither are made to feel guilty. Mother can then go off happily, and the child — relieved of the decision he found it impossible to make — can enter gaily and independently into the life of the nursery school.

There are links with home which no adult should ever sever and which bring ease and security to the child. The hanky in the pocket which mother put there so that it is, in fact, an extension of her; the biscuit or the sweet popped into a mouth that remind the child of mother's special power to love and to give; the small toy; the marble; the bit of towel; the broken pencil; all redolent with the suggestion of home. Sometimes some treasure may be willingly handed over to a trusted and loved teacher to be taken care of, but sometimes these treasures must be held onto firmly all day. Certain rituals and routines may be, for a while, very necessary for the peace of mind of some children, however strange they may appear.

The sudden, sharp, shock of separation may sometimes be inevitable because of a mother's illness or other home crisis. Marian, who had to be left in this way because of her mother's sudden entry to hospital, was dropped hastily at nursery school by an elder sister who, quite naturally, tended to evade Marian's clinging embraces; and she took a long time to settle. At times she seemed happy enough, but at others she cried in heartbreaking snatches and only stopped when she was carried around by someone and comforted. Alice, who had the gentle attention of her mother until she felt really safe, settled in easily and had no setbacks.

Once Peter knew he could cling to his cap all day, he broke away quite easily from his mother after a short period, and she was thankful to leave him as she had a sick husband at home. Came the day when Peter handed his cap over to his beloved teacher to keep for him until he went home. Philip and Mary had to be kissed twice on the doorstep even though their mother had settled them happily at play. Sheila always took something home from nursery school — a pencil, a crayon, a small brick — and as faithfully brought them back next day as if she needed to link together home and nursery school, both places she loved and enjoyed.

Tommy's grandfather was quite angry when his mother stayed for some time to settle Tommy into nursery school gradually.

"Spoiling, that's what I call it," he muttered, "when I went to school any child who cried got the cane and look at me now; did it do me any harm?" Alas, no one could tell Tommy's grandfather what a bad-tempered, morose old man he was. He could not accept the fact that Tommy had a right to feel secure and well loved and that life itself would provide plenty of problems which would have to be endured. The fact that Tommy would be able to face them with greater understanding and fortitude because of the early love and security which he had received did not enter into his thinking.

How did the mothers react to this slow settling in at nursery school? Most of them certainly appreciated it. "I remember I used to have a little cry myself," confessed Mrs. A as she described Charlie's first days at school (he was now a strapping 10-year-old), "I was hustled off the school premises leaving Charlie kicking and screaming with a distracted young teacher who had 29 other 4-year-olds in a baby class, all howling their heads off."

Mrs. Y remembered her own school days; "I escaped from the school on my first day," she said, "and I had to cross a busy road. My mother took me straight back and the teacher had not even missed me. Oh, how I hated going to school every morning!"

Mrs. P was only too thankful she had been able to stay with Ian until he was happily settled. "Maybe I've spoiled him," she said, "but he's always been nervy and delicate and I wouldn't have had a moment's peace if I'd had to leave him crying. He took a long time to settle, but now he just loves it."

Mrs. N felt she was expected to stay too long at the nursery school to settle her twins: "I could have left them the first day," she said, "they didn't want me: still, I expect the teacher was right."

Mrs. D's Mary seemed to settle very quickly — perhaps too quickly, for she had a sudden relapse and cried and clung to her mother. This, however, was probably because of certain tensions and anxieties at home, and when these cleared up Mary seemed to get her confidence back again and let her mother go.

One mother pointed out that children are often asked to bring waste material, etc., from home that the teacher wants for the children to use in making things. Her child Alec tried to explain to his mother what the teacher wanted, but she could not understand what he meant. He was obviously very upset when the other children brought things and he did not. He cried bitterly and did not want to go to nursery school, though he had appeared so happy. When she discovered from the teacher what it was all about, she gave Alec "lots of bits and bobs" and he was as pleased as Punch and could not get to nursery school fast enough.

There is no need to invent difficulties for children, and the more we can do to make their early contacts at nursery school happy and satisfying ones, the better it will be both for the children and their parents.

# CHAPTER 10

# Conclusions

*"Now the great and fatal fruit of our civilization, which is a civilization based on knowledge, and hostile to experience, is boredom. All our wonderful education and learning is producing a grand sum-total of boredom. Modern people are inwardly bored. Do as they may, they are bored. They are bored because they experience nothing. And they experience nothing because the wonder has gone out of them. And when the wonder has gone out of a man he is dead. He is henceforth only an insect. When all comes to all, the most precious element in life is wonder."*
(Fred Inglis, *The Awkward Ages, or What shall we tell the Children?*, Children's Literature in Education, APS Publication No. 13, 1974)

The rôle of the teacher has been considered in relation to various aspects of her work: her relationship with the children and their parents and her nursery assistant; her rather specialized rôle with new entrants and the handicapped child; and the rich, happy, secure atmosphere which she is able to create with her group of children. There are, of course, other aspects of her rôle which are particularly important at the present time, even though they are only mentioned very briefly here. However much we continue to reassess the needs of young children under 5, their essential right to play must be carefully and safely guarded. Play is the breath of life to a young child, and it is only too easy to make inroads on the time children have for this very necessary, enjoyable, and spontaneous activity.

There are, it is true, group experiences which the adult can organize and from which we often feel that young children can learn a great deal. At the same time, however, we must be very careful not to take up valuable time in activities which do not always give children the incentive to develop their own imaginations and their own chosen pleasures. Obviously, story and music periods must be planned, but it is through a child's self-chosen play that so much learning takes place. This is where he is able to make decisions for himself, develop relationships in his own way, and come to

62

terms with the problems and conflicts which life presents to him, and he cannot do this if his play is cut into and constantly interrupted by activities (some of which are so dull) which the teacher thinks children will benefit from. Children must live in the "now" of their childhood – not hurried on to a new stage before they are ready. They need to stand and stare, to absorb an experience and make it their own, and watch the world go by. Time should be *child's* time, for all too soon life's clock catches up with him.

A child who went to a small private nursery school complained to his mother he did not want to go any more – they made him work too hard. His mother eventually discovered what was happening. Whenever he paused to look or listen, to brood quietly over something he had seen and which he was turning over in his mind, an interfering adult came along and interrupted him, asked him what he would like to do, and either tried to persuade him to join a group or presented him with a carefully selected piece of play material, so he had no chance to work things out for himself. Most children possess a marvellous sense of wonder which we do often lose as we get older. There is a feeling of magic in the air, a constant delight in new experiences, life is packed with surprises. This is a quality in children that we must not destroy.

The development of language has taken on an important rôle today, and certainly children need to be able to express themselves in words and communicate in language easily and freely. Obviously, however much a teacher does, her time is limited with a group of 25 children. She will certainly plan all sorts of things and take special care with those children who need more help than others. Perhaps, also, an important rôle that she can play is to help parents to realize how necessary it is for them to talk to their children, to listen to their chatter, answer their questions and share and provide experiences however simple. Many parents, without realizing it, do not listen to their children's conversation and discourage their desire for information. Many homes are devoid of books. They are neither bought nor borrowed, bedtime stories are unknown, and so children have no early pleasure in listening to language through stories and poetry and miss the fun of sharing picture books with their parents.

In summing up, therefore, the teacher's final rôle is to safeguard a. child's right to play, to keep alive in him his sense of wonder, to give him time to enjoy life as he sees it, and to stimulate and encourage his pleasure in language.

# Bibliography

*Books are the masters who instruct us without rods or ferrules,
without hard words and anger, without clothes or money. If you
approach them they are not asleep; if investigating, you interrogate
them they conceal nothing; if you mistake them they never
grumble; if you are ignorant they cannot laugh at you. This feeling
that books are real friends is constantly present to all who love
reading.*
(Richard de Bury, Bishop of Durham, 1344)

ANDERSON, H. H., BREWER, N. M., and REED, M. P., *Studies of Teacher's Classroom Personalities*, I, II, and III, Applied Psychology Monograph, VI, VII, and XI, Stanford University Press, California, 1945–6.

AXLINE, V., *Dibbs in Search of Self*, Victor Gollancz, London, 1966.

BARUCH, D. W., *Parents and Children go to School*, Scott, Foreman & Co., Chicago, 1939.

BOWLBY, J., *Child Care and the Growth of Love*, Penguin Books, London, 1953.

BOYCE, E. R., *The First Year in School*, Nisbet, Glasgow, 1953.

BROWN, C., *My Left Foot*, Martin, Secker & Warburg, London, 1956. *Down All the Days*, Martin, Secker & Warburg, London, 1971.

CARNEGIE TRUST, *Handicapped Children and their Families*, Dunfirmline, 1974.

CASS, J. E., *The Significance of Children's Play*, Batsford, London, 1972.

CURTIS, D. K. and ANDREWS, L., *Guiding Your Student Teacher*, Prentice-Hall, New York, 1957.

FLUGEL, J. C., *The Psycho-analytic Study of the Family*, The Hogarth Press and The Institute of Psycho-analysis, London, 1950.

FRAIBERG, S., *The Magic Years*, Methuen, London, 1968.

GABRIEL, J., *An Analysis of the Emotional Problems of the Teacher in the Classroom*, F. W. Cheshire, Melbourne, 1957.

GARDNER, D. E. M. and CASS, J. E., *The Role of the Teacher in the Infant and Nursery School*, Pergamon Press, Oxford, 1965.

GAVRON, H., *The Captive Wife*, Pelican Books, Hammondsworth, 1968.

GESELL, A. and ILG, F. L., *The Child from Five to Ten*, Hamish Hamilton, London, 1946.

GLASSEY and WEEKES, *The Educational Development of Children*, University of London Press, London, 1958.

HARTLEY, R. E., FRANK, K. L., and GOLDENSON, R. M., *Understanding Children's Play*, Routledge and Kegan Paul, London, 1953.

ISAACS, N., *What is Required of the Nursery Infant Teacher in the Country Today?*, National Froebel Foundation, London, 1957.

# Bibliography

ISAACS, S., *Intellectual Growth in Young Children*, Routledge, London, 1930.
JACKSON, B. and MARSDEN, D., *Education and the Working Class*, Routledge and Kegan Paul, London, 1962.
JACKSON, L. and TODD, M. K., *Child Treatment and the Therapy of Play*, Methuen, London, 1946.
JERSILD, A., *When Teachers Face Themselves*, Teacher's College, Columbia University, 1955.
KELLMER, P. M., *Deprivation and Education*, Longmans, London, 1965. *Emotional and Social Adjustment of the Physically Handicapped*, London 1965.
KLEIN, M. and RIVIERE, J., *Love, Hate and Reparation*, the Hogarth Press and the Institute of Psycho-analysis, London, 1937.
LANDRETH, C., *Education of the Young Child*, Wiley, New York, 1942.
LANE, H. and BEACHAMP, M., *Human Relations in Teaching*, Prentice-Hall, New York, 1955.
MALLINSON, *None Shall be Called Deformed*, Heinemann Books, London, 1956.
MAYS, T. B., *Education of the Urban Child*, Liverpool University Press, 1962.
MCGEENEY, P., *Parents are Welcome*, Longmans, Harlow, 1969.
MELLOR, E., *Education through Experience in the Infant School Years*, Blackwell, Oxford, 1950.
MOH, *Special Education Treatment*, HMSO, London.
NATIONAL UNION OF TEACHERS, *Nursery and Infant Education*, Evans Bros., London, 1950.
NEWSON, J. and NEWSON, E., *Four Years Old in an Urban Community*, Allen & Unwin, London, 1965.
PETERS, J., *Growing Up World*, Longmans, London, 1966.
READ, K. H., *The Nursery School*, Saunders, Philadelphia and London, 1966.
RIDGWAY, L. and LAWTON, I., *Family Grouping in the Infant School*, Ward Lock, London, 1965.
RUSK, R. N., *A History of Infant Education*, University of London Press, 1955.
SCHONELL, F. J., RICHARDSON, J. A., and McCONNEL, S., *The Subnormal Child at Home*, Macmillan, New York, 1958.
THOMAS, J., *Hope for the Handicapped*, Bodley Head, London, 1967.
TIZARD, J., *Community Services for the Mentally Handicapped*, Oxford University Press, London, 1964.
TIZARD, J., *Survey and Experiment in Special Education*, Institute of Education, London, 1967.
TUSTIN, F., *Autism and Childhood Psychosis*, the Hogarth Press, London, 1972.
VERNON, M. D., *The Psychology of Perception*, Penguin Books, Harmondsworth, (reprinted 1973).
WALL, W. D., *Education and Mental Health*, Unesco/Harrap, London, 1955, *Child of Our Time*, National Children's Homes Convocation Lecture, 1959.
WALL, W. D. and FREUD, A., *The Enrichment of Childhood*, Nursery School Association (reprinted 1973).
WHITBREAD, N., *The Evolution of the Nursery–Infant School*, Library of Education, Routledge and Kegan Paul, London, 1972.
WINNICOT, D. W., *The Child, the Family and the Outside World*, Penguin Books, London, 1964.
YOUNG, M. and MCGEENEY, P., *Learning Begins at Home*, Routledge and Kegan Paul, London, 1968.
YOUNGHUSBAND, E., BIRCHALL, D., DAVIS, R., and KELLMER PRINGLE, M. (eds.), *Living with Handicap*, the National Bureau for Co-operation in Child Care, 1970.